Stepfathers' Anonymous Playbook

The Season That Never Ends

Stepfathers' Anonymous Playbook

The Season That Never Ends

Joe Pritchard

COVENANT COMMUNICATIONS

Old Hickory, TN

Stepfathers' Anonymous Playbook
The Season That Never Ends
By: Joe Pritchard

Publisher:

COVENANT
COMMUNICATIONS

P.O. Box 367
Old Hickory, TN 37138-0367

Publisher's Cataloging in Publication
(Prepared by Quality Books Inc.)

Pritchard, Joe M.
     Stepfathers' Anonymous playbook: the season that never ends / Joe Pritchard.
     p. cm.
     ISBN 0-9649122-9-5

1. Stepfathers. 2. Stepfamilies. 3. Family. 4. Parent and child. I. Title.

HQ756.P75 1996   306.874
                                   QBI95-20606

*It is only by forgetting yourself that
you draw near to God.*

Thoreau

With joy I dedicate this book to my wife, Donna,
and my adoptive girls, Shannon and Jamie, who as
my stepchildren, taught me the true meaning of
unconditional love.

Acknowledgments

I would like to thank the following for granting permission to reprint material that is not part of the public domain:

Bobbie Probstein, author of *"The Bag Lady"*, a wonderful Thanksgiving story found on Day # 164.

Excerpts from Dr. Nicholas Hobbs, *"The Art of Getting Into Trouble"*, appear courtesy of Bob Slagle, longtime child advocate and overseer of the Hobbs' library. Bob taught me the meaning of program for success and successful living is healing.

Some scripture taken from the HOLY BIBLE, NEW INTERNATIONAL VERSION. Copyright 1973, 1978, 1984 by International Book Society. Used by permission of Zondervan Publishing House.

Unless noted all scripture is from the King James version of the Bible.

Numerous others contributed to this book... first and foremost, my wife, Donna, who just happens to also be my business partner, best friend, and family referee. Without her encouragement, patience, and willingness to feed the family and keep a roof over our heads, this project, not to mention Covenant Communications, would still be a dream. Folks like Penny Wheeler, editor at the Review & Herald and longtime friend, who provided countless hours of consultation, Sandra Self of Graphics Unlimited for her work on the ever-changing manuscript, and my mom and brothers, Tom and Bob, who provided encouragement and endured hours of proofreading.

A special thanks to Shawn Bullard, who designed the cover; Albert Douglas, our illustrator, Josh and the folks at Word Mill Prepress for "reprogramming" the mess I gave them on disc, and Tom and the crew at Patterson Printing.

Contents

Preface

In the past four years I have experienced the joys and the sorrows of stepparenting. This book is about those experiences. The anecdotes involving my family are based on truth. My two teenage stepdaughters and my wife provided the material. I simply added the humor... humor that was not necessarily present at the time of the actual events. It's much easier looking back and laughing at ourselves.

Regarding the stepfather groups that I write about, the stories are true... the characters real. However, the group meetings are fictional. I simply pulled the various stepfamily scenarios I had dealt with over the years as a counselor into a group format. My dream is that men of vision and courage will take this notion of stepfathers bonding together and "put it into play."

I hope this book offers some insight, hope, and humor for the millions of stepparents already out there "in the arena" as well as for the half-million souls who join the blended family game every year.

Foreword

I have known Joe Pritchard for many years and worked with him much of that time in a very close relationship. He is an excellent therapist whose judgment is impeccable and whose ability to reach people impressed me from the very beginning. I had no idea, however, that he was a writer!

When Joe asked me to do the foreword to his book, *Stepfathers' Anonymous Playbook... The Season That Never Ends*, I was at best skeptical. Why would anyone write a book about stepfathers and their unique problems? What's so exciting about this? It happens every day with fifty percent of the marriages in this country. Indeed, I am a stepfather, having reared two boys from just prior to puberty up until the time they "flew the nest." Therefore, it was with some hesitation that I agreed to read the book and write the foreword.

I began reading the book and found that I could not put it down! It can be comfortably read in one night. I felt myself hit in the face with practical, down-to-earth suggestions and advice, a wry sense of humor which I did not know Joe possessed, and an engaging storyline interspersed with Biblical text which lended validity to the total substance of the book.

Joe found himself for the first time the stepfather to two young ladies just coming into maturity. What was to transpire in his new relationship was a revelation to him which he has cleverly and professionally put into proper perspective. His daily accounts of the problems, trials and tribulations, and successes outline what every stepfather has experienced. In my own experience, I found myself reluctant to correct two stepchildren as I had done my biological children, and Joe encountered similar problems with the issue of discipline. His practical approach points out, however, that the stepfather has to step in and tend to the discipline and correction of his stepchildren. Further, he points out very succinctly that the mother (his wife) and he have to be in one accord as to what should be done and be allowed and be disciplined with the children. It struck me again in the face that this is exactly what happens with one's biological children as well.

When the problems arise day-by-day, Joe brings the problems into proper focus along with an occasional belly laugh. His thought for the day often quotes famous individuals whose wisdom is imparted to the book. He has also carefully selected related Scriptures to support his thoughts.

I feel the "Stepfathers' Anonymous groups" where men struggling with stepparenting issues could ventilate and share experiences were the most valuable aspect of his book. As a psychiatrist for many years, I found when people are willing in a group setting to state the problems and the thoughts they have kept to themselves over the years and find out that others have identical problems, they instantly feel better and realize that they're not "crazy" and they are not alone. Joe has done an excellent job of presenting the group meetings in both an entertaining as well as enlightening fashion. The notion of stepfathers meeting weekly is an engaging idea and one that should be pursued. I know Joe is excited about starting Stepfathers' Anonymous groups around the country in the coming years. With his firsthand experiences and natural people skills, I'm sure stepfathers will be giving up their "Lazy Boys" and TV buttons routinely to meet and share their stories.

The message of the book is timeless. It will be accurate for years to come as it has been for years in the past. There are no profound discoveries… just common sense, down-to-earth approaches to problems that arise as stepfamilies are joined together under one roof.

I suspect you will have a difficult time putting the book down. I also suspect you will have a hearty belly laugh or two as you venture into the Pritchard household. Finally, I suspect you will reflect soberly on the overall content and message of the book.

I highly recommend that all parents and adult children of stepfamilies read *Stepfathers' Anonymous Playbook… The Season That*

Never Ends. It's a rare book that can enlighten and entertain you in one sitting, yet entice you to read over and over. It's a comedy, a touching story, a diary/textbook and a devotional book rolled into one. Enjoy it!

Nat T. Winston, M.D.
Chairman, CareNet Health Systems
Former Commissioner of Mental
Health for the state of Tennessee

The journey of a thousand miles begins with a single step....

1

in the beginning

In the beginning God created the heavens and the earth… And God said, Let us make man in our own image after our own likeness… so God created man in his own image of God created he him; male and female created he them.
                                        Genesis 1:1, 26-27

Try not become a man of success,
Rather become a man of value.
                                        Albert Einstein

In the beginning God created the heavens and the earth… and man and woman. His initial plans did not call for divorce and suffering. However, Eve proved early in the game that men were gullible and easy marks with huge egos. Thus, with the inevitable decline and fall of the nuclear family, God decided to make the best of a rather sad situation by allowing a new breed of men to emerge from the ruins – Stepfathers… if at first you don't succeed, you give it another shot. In some cases two shots may not be enough.

This new breed would be men of vision, unafraid of their predecessors and years of failure. They would band together in large packs throughout the universe… real men eating quiche and working out with Jane Fonda as they cited the Stepfathers' Anonymous Creed:

> I am a stepfather. I was born to be a father. Regardless of my past path I can be a positive role model for my children. I do possess the inner strength and God-given capabilities to lead my children down the path of righteousness, world without end, and it may take till the end. I also am a man, descendant of the first great failure, Adam. However, I was re-created by God in His own image and do possess the God-given capabilities to serve my wife faithfully and humbly. I can faithfully serve my new family with dignity and honor without the assistance of illicit substances or any illicit behavior, including that horrible creature known as TVbutt. I will find alternative uses for my button pushing hand. I also fully accept the responsibility of knowing that I may not be able to handle social button pushing. I would benefit from abstinence of all vices, given that my biological makeup is geared to the old man's ways of failure and neglect of family duty. I am committed to the above mentioned values and prepared to take this message to the ends of the earth,

not to mention my willingness to contact my brothers if I feel myself succumbing to my biological desires to eat, drink, and do nothing for nobody. I am one of the new breed. I am a member of Stepfathers' Anonymous.

Amen.

Along with this new breed came a Stepfathers' Anonymous handbook. It seemed the original handbook handed down by Almighty God, otherwise known as the Bible, or in Stepfathers' Anonymous lingo, affectionately referred to as The Word… it seemed original man failed to follow God's instructions regarding studying The Word. Wheel of Fortune and The Dirty Dozen reruns took over until the advent of TVbutt and ESPN. Somewhere in the midst The Word got lost. As a result the kids, the wife, everything got lost.

The Stepfathers' Anonymous handbook, known as the SFA Playbook, was created to work in conjunction with The Word. It was never intended as a substitute for the Bible and should not be used as such. Its sole purpose is to serve as a guide to keep stepfathers on the path to the FeatherZone. That is what SFA members affectionately refer to as heaven on earth. According to a select few SFA enlightened souls, the FeatherZone is obtainable prior to retirement or Alzheimer's, whichever comes first. However, those select few who have reached the FeatherZone are quick to point out that they found heaven on earth by maintaining an unwavering commitment to the following:

1) Daily devotional time with God, the ultimate Father, and His Word;

2) Lifelong, daily commitment to forgive others of any wrongdoings and to seek the true meaning of unconditional love as exemplified by Jesus Christ;

3) Lifelong, daily commitment to bring some measure of joy, no matter how small or brief, into the lives of their kids and their wives;

4) Lifelong, <u>daily</u> commitment to maintain a healthy balance between work and family, and in no way, shape, or form allow work to take precedence over what truly matters most... family;

5) <u>Daily</u> recital of the Serenity Prayer, along with supplemental reading on an as needed basis of the SFA Playbook.

May the Power of God and His Word be with you on your journey...

All I have seen teaches me to trust the
Creator for all I have not seen.
Ralph Waldo Emerson

The ultimate measure of a man is not where he stands in
moments of comfort and convenience, but where he
stands at times of challenge and controversy.
Martin Luther King, Jr.

Life is truly meant to be shared with someone you love....

paradise lost

paradise: from Greek *paradeisos*... **1.** Heaven. **2.** a place or state of bliss. **3.** Holden Beach, North Carolina... late September, high tide, sun setting in the west and full moon just above the horizon to the east; 19 pelicans flying in formation a foot above the pounding waves... not another human being in sight.

lost: 1. unable to find the way. **2.** the absence of a soulmate to share the wonder with...

I was thirty-seven years old and free again, having divorced a year earlier from a five year, no children marriage. We had decided not to have kids for the first three years of our marriage, opting to enjoy our freedom. During the last two years of the marriage, we started doubting our stability, knowing that kids should not be brought into this world under such a cloud of uncertainty. Thus, we parted our ways, and I left town to pursue another job and a new life.

The Good Lord introduced me to paradise here on earth. I was managing an adolescent psychiatric unit on the North Carolina coast and living on the ocean. The hospital was only seven miles from my place on the beach. Nine months out of the year I rarely passed but a handful of cars going to work. I took long walks on the beach, at times communicating only with seagulls and pelicans. The beach was deserted.

On this particular beach from late fall to early spring, I could see both a sunrise and a sunset over the water. Many a late afternoon I watched the sun setting in the west while the moon majestically appeared over the horizon to the east... dolphin playfully swimming a mere 100 yards from the shoreline... the rhythmic sounds of the ocean waves forever playing on.

Needless to say I fell in love with the ocean. I had always had a fascination with the beach as a child even though our family rarely had the opportunity to go. Now, as a 37-year-old divorced male with no kids and no real ties beyond a beeper, I was in paradise. Even during the hectic summer season the beach maintained a quiet majesty about itself. And if I wanted excitement, Myrtle Beach was a mere forty minute cruise down the coast. I seemed to have it all, yet the feeling was beginning to emerge.

Professionally, I had moved up in the world, leaving behind twelve long years of working with emotionally disturbed children in state hospitals and agencies. I was now working for a private corporation. Dressed for success I was occasionally flown to corporate headquarters, other hospital sites, corporate Christmas parties... I felt important. I felt like somebody. But the feelings of emptiness were getting stronger.

I vividly remember flying home for Christmas that year to my mom's house and returning to the beach on the night of December 26th to attend a hospital department head party. The pilot had mentioned a record snowfall, but little did I know the magnitude of such until I stepped off the sidewalk at the Wilmington airport, only to find the snow came to my knees.

It was the following morning that I so vividly recall. I woke up, looked out the window, and saw the beach covered with snow and dolphin gracefully swimming fifty yards off shore. It was low tide and the ocean was unusually quiet that morning. It was a sight I'll never forget and a feeling I'll long remember... complete emptiness. Here I was witnessing one of the most spectacular sights on God's earth, and I had no one to share it with. I had never felt such loneliness in all my life.

I was used to being a loner. I was not the type person who wanted or needed people around. I always preferred the crowds from a distance, watching but not necessarily interacting with its members. On that serene morning with the snow-covered beach and no one in sight, I was not suffering from the absence of humanity. The dolphin were great company. What I suffered from was the lack of a loved one... a soulmate to share the marvel with me. I was grateful that God had connected me with the ocean. My love affair with the beach would be eternal. However, I realized that life was truly meant to be shared with someone you love.

My first wife of five years was a wonderful human being... good natured, easy going. But, as I continued to live on the ocean over the next year and reflect on my failed marriage, I realized that I still had not experienced true love, whatever that truly was. I wondered if I ever would experience it with a woman... unconditional, unabridged love and acceptance like I felt for the ocean... rain or shine, summer or winter, day or night.

I was living in paradise lost. It was only a matter of time before I would leave. The isolation had become too much to bear. I had seen paradise and knew that someday I would return. I needed to move on for sanity's sake.

For someone who had lived in the same town from birth to age thirty-six, I was now preparing to move again for the second time in a year. I was given the opportunity to move to Nashville and start a new pediatric psych unit. I was ready for the change professionally. I had stabilized the once-shaken adolescent unit at the beach and was ready to move away from the always turbulent teenage units to younger kids whose temper outbursts were more readily controlled. Thus, after a year of beach time, I was moving back into civilization, heading for the music city capital of the world — Nashville.

After a week of circling the city, I finally found my way around town and moved into a nice, two-bedroom apartment. For the first time in my life I was out-of-debt and making a good salary. I splurged and bought new furniture for the entire place, including a washer and dryer.

I was excited about the washer and dryer. Throughout most of my adult life, I had experienced the intimate joys of laundry mats and university housing washerettes. Now, I had it all! What a novelty… I could wash and dry my clothes and never leave my apartment!

I was rich! Money in my pocket, new furniture, a nice apartment with a fireplace… I was ready to tackle the single life again. I knew that, God willing, I would return to my true love someday — the ocean. However, the loneliness appeared to be lifting, and I was ready to do some two-steppin and experience the good life.

Little did I know that God had another course of action for me.

The heart has its reasons which reason knows nothing of.
Pascal

We know not what the future holds,
but we do know Who holds the future.
Anonymous

3

exhibition season

exhibit: 1. to display, especially publicly. **2.** to put one's strongest foot forward when wading in turbulent waters with a fishing pole and no line.

hooked: 1. to seize or make fast with a hook. **2.** when your girlfriend's daughters and your girlfriend join forces to reel you in.

December 26th

Another Christmas gone by... My 37th on this earth. This particular Christmas was different. My mom's house was not quite as crowded as in year's past. You see, two of her sons had divorced earlier in the year, and her grandkids from her oldest son's marriage were not present. Neither were my mom's two former daughter-in-laws, one of which was my ex-wife. We had no children.

My mother tried to hide the sadness, but I knew it was there. Perhaps she sensed the sadness in me. After all, Christmas morning is not meant to be spent alone. It is to be shared with loved ones and with children running around dazed with anticipation and excitement. Sure, I was at my mom's with my two older brothers. But, it just wasn't the same. "God must be punishing me for not taking my first marriage to heart," I thought to myself. I was used to being alone but not this alone.

I'm sure not planning on jumping into anything soon. The single life will suit me again as it had done for the first thirty-one years of my life. I'll get back into the swing of things when I get back home to Nashville and my new apartment. I've got a new life ahead of me, and I'm going to make something positive happen starting January 1st. Until then, I will continue on my current downward course. I know God will watch out for me until I get my act together. He always has been there.

It is quiet as I start back home. I can see my mom's face in the distance, worrying about her 37-year-old "baby" son. I can sense God's presence too, also concerned about this lost child wondering in the wilderness.

And the birth of His Son, Jesus... what Christmas is supposed to be all about. I keep wondering what it must be like to have a son...

January 1st

The bowl games and parades don't mean much anymore, at least not as much when you watch them by yourself. I made no New Year's resolutions last night. I just went out and forgot about how lonely I was inside.

It may take a few days but I know I'll get started back on the right path. I always manage to…

Meanwhile, my new TVbutt works great, almost as fast changing channels as my mom's. I can watch the Orange Bowl and the Sugar Bowl virtually at the same time, and there's no one here to fuss at me about playing with the buttons or lying on my rear end and not moving. Maybe this single life will be okay. I don't even have to answer the phone; just let the machine take care of it. Outside of work, I don't have to listen to anybody… I don't have to be anybody.

Thought for the Day: Why black-eyed peas… and does it count if they come from a can?

January 8th

I'm finally back on track! I've started back on my exercise program and my diet has improved… thank goodness for fast food health foods!

I saw a woman at the hospital today who sure turned my head and made my heart flutter. She was a pretty blonde about 5'2" and built like… well, like God intended woman to be built when He created her from Adam's rib.

Meanwhile, it's time for another treatment of Color My Gray — it works as long as you don't leave it on too long.

I don't think she is married. I did not see a wedding band. I'll send a scout out tomorrow to gather details.

January 11th

I haven't seen her in several days now. I'm wondering what happened. Did my dream girl just up and disappear?

If she did, I'll survive. After all, this is a big town with lots of fish out there waiting to be caught. The problem with me is I never liked fishing. Oh, I've always enjoyed going out in the waters, but when it comes to throwing a line I'm not real good and frankly, I don't enjoy it.

Maybe I'll try one of those video dating... No, that's not me either. Besides, why am I so hung up on meeting someone and getting involved? It has been a year since my divorce and haven't I enjoyed the freedom? When I leave work I can do whatever I want as long as I keep my beeper within earshot. That's the only thing I need to be married to — my beeper, my job. Otherwise, I'm free to come and go as I please and with whomever I please. What more could a guy ask for? I've got a new apartment with new furniture, new clothes, money in my pocket, and no real responsibility outside of work.

January 12th

Why am I so lonely? The weekend has arrived. What am I going to do? There's a group from work going out... Nah, I see enough of them during the week. Besides, they truly don't interest me. I'll just stay in and continue getting my new place in order. After all, my exercise program is going well as is my diet. I don't want to lose ground there. Who knows... I may run out somewhere Saturday night. I'm learning my way around town and know a few places to go fishing.

Why am I always thinking about finding a woman? It's as if something inside of me keeps gnawing at me, telling me life without woman is dead. Is that true? I love the company of a good woman, yet I enjoy being alone.

I miss sharing movies and ideas with a woman, yet I'm not sure

I'm ready to have someone around all the time.

Prayer: Hear me, God… I'm confused. Lead me down the path of righteousness. I've strayed so many times, yet I've never lost faith in Your kindness and compassion… Your willingness to pick me up and guide me. I need your guidance now. Show me the way, the truth… the light.

January 16th

I saw her again this morning. Her long, curly blonde hair glistened in the light. Her eyes appeared blue, although I was afraid to look very long for fear that she knew. I've got to meet her but how? I'm so afraid and yet, so excited… What a feeling!

January 18th

Contact! Yes, I did have it in me to speak. Her name is Donna, and as my scout had informed me last week she is divorced. Small world, huh?

January 19th

The weekend again… Why didn't I ask her out? Why was I so afraid? She seemed interested. Am I that afraid of rejection or failure? Here I sit in my rented kingdom, alone again with TVbutt… the buttons don't even mean much unless you've got someone to share the clicking sound with you… of course, as long as you have the buttons!

Somehow, I must muster the courage and intestinal fortitude to ask her out. Too many more weekends in this kingdom of mine and…

It's time to go fishing...

Thought for the Day: Loneliness is a funny creature. It forces you to look at yourself... to self-analyze yourself — That is, if you can put TVbutt down long enough to deal with the reality around you. It's very easy to come home from work and self-stim the night away... never watching any one program for more than ten seconds at a time. Given that scenario I switched channels 1800 times tonight... 1800 times I pounded that magic button. Oh, what a thrill... a mindless thrill. I know people paying $70/hour who don't get as good a therapy as I give myself.

January 22nd

I don't know where it came from, but I mustered the guts to ask her out and she said yes! Specific plans to be set later...
I'm scared to death!

January 26th

Our first date. She came to my place for dinner... how 'bout that! I fixed vegetarian casserole since she forewarned me that she did not eat meat or fish. Thank goodness I had experienced a vegetarian diet back in my college days — it didn't bother me in the least.

Going to church on Saturday? Now that was different. But, I could live with it as long as I could sneek a peek at the college football scores, and by all means, stay home from church every third Saturday in October when Tennessee played Alabama. After all, that was a sacred Saturday every year... a Southern tradition... Bear Bryant, Neyland Stadium with 95,000 fans. Surely Donna had heard of the Bear?

Our evening was enjoyable. We ate and went out afterwards. We had a good time, but I was somewhat taken back that Donna knew nothing about the Bear. In fact, she knew nothing about sports! A home run might as well have been a two-point conversion in her playbook.

She had grown up on a farm… climbing trees, feeding the animals, working with her father in the great outdoors from dawn to dusk. He didn't care much for television except to watch an occasional western or Bonanza rerun. Otherwise, he was outside in the fresh air tinkering with his horses.

Needless to say, we were as different as night and day, and yet, there was something in Donna that I could not get out of my head. I liked her… very much. No, this wasn't me responding to the first woman to come down the pike. Yeah, I had been lonely and was growing tired of spending weekends alone, but there was something special about Donna. I can't put my finger on it yet, but in due time I will.

Oh yeah, Donna has two kids she is raising full-time since her divorce. Two teenage daughters… I'm going to meet them next week.

January 29th

I went to Donna's for dinner after work and met her family. Shannon just turned sixteen while Jamie was fourteen. They seemed like nice kids to me. Jamie was a spitting image of her mom; they looked like sisters. Shannon was somewhat aloof but not in the least bit disrespectful. She simply appeared to be checking me out a little more than Jamie, perhaps sensing that her mom was more than just casually interested in me… "Why else would she invite this man over to eat with us? We never actually sit down at the same time anymore and eat a meal. Why are we pretending that such an event takes place every night?"

February 25th

The courting continues… The more I see of Donna the more I like. She is different. She grew up differently than I did. We're continuing to discover little nuances about each other, some irritating, yet insignificant in terms of the big picture. We enjoy each other's company and spiritually we're in the same ballpark. In fact, Donna is bringing me back to the basics of the Bible… something I've needed and longed for.

In the past ten years my faith in God and belief in Jesus Christ had remained constant. I no longer had my doubts or fears. But, my day-to-day spiritual path had been rocky and often times misguided. Donna was re-introducing me to the simple foundation of the Bible and I was enjoying the journey.

I was also enjoying the vision of a family… my family. For the first time I was imagining myself as head of a household; me, Donna, Shannon, Jamie, and of course, Chelsey and Kendra… the two female dogs that Donna had found on the streets sometime ago.

It seems she had a real soft place for throw-away animals and a more hardened heart for throw-away (homeless) people. I was just the opposite. My heart always went out to the lonely, downtrodden human on the side of the road. Homeless dogs? My fingers did the walking to the dog catcher's telephone number. Pets were a nuisance… a responsibility I didn't need. However, I was learning to get along with the two muts for the sake of image if nothing else.

Back to the vision of head of the household… I could see it happening. After all, Donna and I were compatible. We had seen quite a bit of each other over the past few months. Surely that was enough time to determine… WHOA! I said WHOA! Things are happening way too fast here. Back up my friend. Stop the vision! Stop the music. You've got to be delusional, right? After all, you just moved here three months ago. You're locking down on this one relationship without giving yourself the chance to see the world again. What about freedom? What about no responsibility? What about her kids? And those dogs...

March 19th

My 38th birthday... Too late, I'm hooked. Read the following from the homemade birthday card that Jamie sent me...

> *Dear Joe,*
>
> *Hey, what's happening? Hope you have a nice birthday today and all your dreams come true. My mom sure does like you and I do too. You've been great to have around and well, I hope you're always going to be around. You would make a cool dad to have.*
>
> > *Love,*
> > *Jamie*

I'm going to be a stepfather. I can feel it in my bones...

The Art of Getting Into Trouble

Life is always highly problematic and what you become will rest in no small measure on the kinds of problem situations you get yourself into and have to work yourself out of. It is exceedingly difficult for a person to take thought and alter the quality and character and direction of his life. However, he can choose the direction he would like his life to take and then put himself deliberately in situations that will require the evaluation of himself toward the kind of person he would like to become.

It is deep in the nature of man to make problems for himself. Man has often been called the problem-solver but he is even more the problem-maker. Every noble achievement of men — in government, art, architecture, literature, and above all, in science represents a new synthesis of the human experience, deepening our understanding and enriching our spirit....

To know a person, it is useful to know what he has done, another way of defining what problems he has solved. It is even more informative, however, to know what problems he is working on now. For these will define the growing edge of his being.

We sometimes think of the well adjusted person as having very few problems, while, in fact, just the opposite is true. When a person is ill or injured or crushed with grief or deeply frightened, the range of his concerns become sharply constricted; his problems diminish in scope and quality.

By contrast, the healthy person, the person healthy in body and mind and spirit, is a person faced with many difficulties. He has a lot of problems, many of which he has deliberately chosen with the sure knowledge that in working toward their solution, he will become more the person he would like to be.

Part of the art of choosing difficulties is to select those that are indeed just manageable. If the difficulties chosen are too easy life is boring; if too hard, life is self-defeating. The trick is to move oneself in the direction of what he would like to become at a level of difficulty close to the edge of his competence. When one achieves this fine tuning of his life, he will know zest and joy and deep fulfillment.

Nicholas Hobbs

"Benched"

4

let the games begin

step-fa-ther: 1. one who is frequently stepped on; dumped on with enormous amounts of displaced anger. **2.** frequently set up by children of a lesser god who utilize massive amounts of manipulation to inflict emotional bombs and blitzes. **3.** an adult male attempting to fill a biological void that is impossible to replace. **4.** a coach seeking the ultimate endurance test of turnovers and misplaced equipment, not to mention clothes, shaving cream… you name it.

step-fa-ther: 1. another adult who is likely to run out on us; who considers us part of the package deal. **2.** one who can never truly love us for ourselves… who will shove us aside the minute his biological children show up, or worse — decides to have a monster of his own with our mother! **3.** a man who will monopolize our mother's time to the point that we eventually lose her too. **4.** one who can't wait for us to grow up and get out of his hair, not to mention his stuff.

Life is change…
Growth is optional.
Choose wisely.

Prayer: O Lord, give me strength to endure this season to be filled with many joys and pitfalls. Give me patience, kindness, and courage in the face of screaming kids, barking dogs, and telephones ringing at all hours of the night. Teach me to bite my tongue in the midst of my anger… never to unleash a barrage of cutting words towards my fragile stepdaughters, who so desperately need a positive, male role model in their lives. Teach me to be humble in my new bride's presence, never to gloat over spilt milk or lost articles of my clothing… especially my socks. Help me to let go of the significance of material items like my stereo and twenty year music collection. Heavenly Father, above all, teach me the true meaning of unconditional love and how to share it with my new family every day, just as You display Your unconditional love to me.

Our wedding day… opening season. Let's play two ala Ernie Banks. Nothing fancy, not even a packed house in the chapel, but what a beautiful day to start the season. Definitely no rain delays today!

I had a great opening day… two hits, scored three times, no kids and no errors. It's going to be a great season! I can feel it in my bones… Not bad for a 38-year-old rookie stepfather.

Day # 2 Reality Bites and Sometimes Stinks…

The honeymoon is over. Reality has a way of smacking you in the face. We returned to the house to find an absolute mess. Apparently, the girls ignored the dogs' pleas to relieve themselves. The basement is deep… Apparently, the girls ignored just about everything in the house today because they were gone when we returned from our one night honeymoon and next day hike in the mountains.

Clothes everywhere, dishes and food left out, the air conditioning on while windows left wide open… It's going to be a long season. The girls did leave us a note…

Mom & Dad,

> *Hope you had a good time. Amy came by and we've gone to the mall. Be home around nine tonight.*

> > *Love,*
> > *Shannon & Jamie*

They called me "Dad". I've never been called that before. It feels pretty good! Meanwhile, the basement calls…

Fatherhood has a distinct smell to it.

The maturity of man — to have reacquired the seriousness he had as a child at play.
Nietzsche

Day # 3 Family Feud…

Our first real argument, full blown just three days into the season. The clubhouse was rocking today. Naturally, I assumed the role of manager/coach. After all, I had been directing traffic since I was a skinny-legged seventh grader playing point guard on the basketball team and shortstop on the baseball team.

I was accustomed to taking charge in many situations, especially those involving kids. I was the 12-year veteran of the state hospital wards with the meanest, toughest, most disturbed kids around. I was the successful manager of kid psych units over the past four years. I knew what I was doing.

Little did I know...

Prayer: Humble me, O Father. Beseech me to learn to keep my mouth shut and let the biological mother put her foot in her mouth. Help me to come to the realization that when engaging in teenage warfare, the enemy has absolutely no concept of reality as perceived by anyone over the age of twenty-five. Most importantly, help me to look beneath the outward behavior that is on display. Teach me to interpret their true feelings... sense their innermost insecurities and fears about my presence in their lives. Teach me to love them for who they are, no matter how much they intend to shock me with their behavior. Above all, make me understand that family arguments are not about winning and losing. At this stage, they're about searching for security and boundaries... and unconditional love/acceptance as human beings.

Father, I know all these things... I know in my heart what's going on. Help me to take a step back and "see" with my heart. Otherwise, my head is about to explode, and I'm ready to bench the entire team for insubordination. Problem is I don't know who the second team is — the dogs have already been benched!

Day # 4 Make-up Game

I'm beginning to learn how my stepdaughters and my new bride deal with stress. Of course, I've dealt with stress all my life, took courses on stress management, mastered the art of relaxation exercises... I can deal with the cards that have been dealt can't I?

It is utterly amazing to me that my oldest daughter, Shannon, and her mom can have a major argument, almost coming to blows, and within fifteen minutes behave around each other as if nothing ever happened. I've never seen anything like it in my life — an amazing ability to forget; at least on Shannon's part. My wife doesn't actually forget the episode. She... well, I'm not sure what she actually does yet.

41

Shannon, on the other hand, either totally forgets it, or is wasting her time and should go straight to Hollywood and apply for an Oscar. I'm not sure where the truth lies at this stage of our development. Shannon is dramatic though, no question about it.

Jamie, my youngest, is sensitive. She runs when the screaming starts. She withdraws to her room, turns on the music, and tunes out for awhile... until later that night when she slides a letter under our door...

Mom/Dad (I love that name!)

Hey, what's happening? I'm sorry I got so mad tonight (I didn't know she did I was so focused on the battle between Shannon and her mom). *You see...* Then she proceeds to explain her version of the scenario as only a fourteen-year-old can do. She ends her note with... *P.S. Hey dad, think we could go to a ball game some time?*

Man, she just melted me on the spot! Jamie has either figured out my soft side real fast or we think an awful lot alike.

Day # 7 Where's My Uniform?

I know I had six good pair of dark socks, one for each day of the week and one pair for church. It's Tuesday and I'm down to two pair, neither of which are mates. The white socks I use for working out are all gone, vanished into thin air without a trace. No one seems to know where they go when asked. Of course, neither of my girls has worn them, especially the white socks. My wife has been trying to convince me for days that washers and dryers are notorious for eating socks.

Have you ever heard of a sock eating washer or dryer? I've done my clothes for seventeen years, and I've yet to lose a sock to either one. Why all of a sudden?

And my shirts... I'm missing at least three shirts! I know I'm an obsessive/compulsive individual who keeps only enough clothing around to get by on — five to six dress shirts and pants for work, one pair of dress shoes… that's about it. The rest are jeans and sweat shirts. When it comes to dress clothes, I don't know half the time what shirt goes with what pair of pants and tie, thus I like to keep it simple… and organized!

My underwear is all there — Nope, there's one pair missing of that too. Wait a minute… What are the odds that the kids?

I found the missing underwear and three socks — none mates of course… behind the dryer. I guess I had better check behind these clothes eating monsters every week.

Meanwhile, I wonder what Donna would think about locks on our bedroom door, provided, of course, she doesn't have to worry about finding the key. Me? I never lose my keys or personal items.

Prayer: God, grant me the patience to live with these imperfect people; to let go of my petty compulsons regarding trivial items like socks and underwear. Help me to better understand how their minds think, given that all three have no concept of orderliness as I have known it. Teach me to love them for who they are, not what they do. Teach me the true meaning of love, Father. I'm just now beginning to see that I have no real concept of what unconditional love is all about.

Help me…

Day # 9 In the Middle of the Road…

Donna cannot win in this situation. No matter which way she turns, someone is waiting to say, "You're not being fair to me."

If I do something wrong or snap at the kids because it's my time of the month, she tries to cover for me and take the heat. She obviously loves me very much — anyone willing to take the heat from those two is either a glutton for punishment or truly in love.

However, the reciprical is true as well. If the kids do something wrong and I confront them, she covers for the kids. She takes the heat for them too, and I can dish out some heat when angry… that is if you can get me going. All too often I simply shut down. Then Donna is back to covering for me. She must enjoy switching roles so abruptly. I think the kids and I must have a subconscious evil side that manufactures verbal garbage at each other, only to watch Donna zoom back and forth between protector of each… like a puppet on a string.

She's a good woman, that Donna. She sures loves her kids and me too. Under the same roof, that's a pretty tough role to carry out day after day, and we're only two weeks into the season.

Maybe we better check her out in six months to see if she's still hitting on all cylinders.

Speaking of cylinders I took the girls driving tonight. Actually, we took my old five-speed Subaru up to the church parking lot, and I let the girls practice driving while I shot some hoops. I can still knock the lights out from twenty feet! Problem is the girls about knocked the lights out of the church building at one point — Shannon, the oldest did anyway. I was surprised how fast Jamie picked up on working the clutch, shifting gears… not bad for a 14-year-old. I wondered if she had driven a straight shift before.

Little did I know what the neighbor would tell us about a month later…

Thought for the Day: If your wife swears that her 14-year-old daughter has never driven a straight shift before, and you notice the first time you take her out driving she handles the stick/clutch cleanly, what does that tell you? Whose car? And when?

Sometimes looking deep into the eyes of a child, you are conscious of meeting a glance full of wisdom. The child has known nothing yet but love and beauty. All this piled-up world knowledge you have acquired is

unguessed by him. And yet, you meet this wonderful look
that tells you in a moment more than all the years of
experience have seemed to teach.
                                    Hildegarde Hawthorne

There is more of good nature than of good sense at the
bottom of most marriages.
                                                   Thoreau

Day # 15 History Lesson…

I can see my father so clearly now. I was fifteen years old and
starting to grow a mustache…emulating one of my heroes, Joe Willie
Namath. My dad hit the ceiling, even though he quietly admired
Namath's grit and style. I stopped growing it… as if I could actually
grow one anyway — nothing more than a conglomeration of peach
fuzz.

At nineteen while playing baseball for the University of Tennessee, I really rebelled. I let my hair grow as long as the coach would
allow, and I grew a real mustache. It was the spring of '72. Woodstock
had come and gone, but everybody on campus, including us "jocks",
was searching for nirvana. Some found it in sociology class. Others
found it in the student center. Still others went searching in the off-
campus chemistry labs that seemed to be on every corner. The times
they were a changin…

At the age of seventeen in the summer of '92, my oldest daughter
was taking me on a trip back in time. I came home early from work
one day and thought I had stepped back into 1972. The Doors were
blaring on the stereo… make that my stereo. I could hear it as I turned
the corner into the neighborhood.

When I made my way beyond the usual household mess at that

45

time of the day — the time when the kids were home from school and we were not scheduled to be home for another hour or so (it took about two weeks to figure out that the girls threw everything in the closets about five minutes before our arrival)… Anyway, I found my daughter dressed in some type of garb that would have made the original hippies proud. She just smiled and said, "Hi dad."

If my father could only see me now…

Thought for the Day: What goes around, comes around.

Prayer: Heavenly Father, why do you allow our offspring to repeat the same mistakes… to wind up on the same paths? It must be awfully boring for You and Your heavenly host of angels knowing that every 25 years or so history, from a cultural explosion standpoint, simply repeats itself with a new generation of rebellious youth. Your patience and sense of humor astound me. Most of all, your willingness to always look into someone's heart to find meaning and truth. Teach me to get better at that. Teach me to see with the heart…

Day # 21 What Will Others Think?

Three weeks into the season and we're still hanging tough. We're not in first place, but we're not in the cellar either. No one is hollering for the manager's head so I must be doing okay, assuming I am the coach. I'm not sure yet. Donna wants me to think and feel like I'm in charge, but the reality is this — when all heck breaks loose, Donna takes over. Of course, Shannon, our seventeen-year-old, thinks she's in charge.

Don't tell anyone but Chelsey, the BIG throwaway dog that Donna and the kids found on the side of the road scared to death during a storm, gets my vote. When she barks I listen. Otherwise, I know what will be waiting for me in the basement later.

The girls are starting to compete a little bit for my attention. Both have already figured out how to butter both sides of my bread. And I thought I was tough! Too much of my father in me… a real "softie" deep down inside.

Shannon enjoys watching movies and occasionally striking up a highly controversial conversation on topics such as staying out all night with friends at Dragon Park (local campus hippie hangout) and "philosophizing." Shannon must have told her latest boyfriend that I worked with kids. When I asked him the other night what he wanted to be, he told me he was going to college to study to become a "socioologist." I thought I knew what a sociologist was all about; I'm not so sure about a socioologist. Then again, I'm not so sure about the boyfriend either. He looks like he walked off the streets of London with his combat boots, partially shaved head, earrings… need I say more?

I keep having these flashbacks to my parents. My mom was always big on the concept, "What will other people think?" In other words, don't do anything outlandish to draw attention… People might think… That concept was drilled into my head. It's still there today, although my girls are definitely loosening me up. I was not loosened up enough, however, for what happened at church.

Shannon decided to bring her socioologist boyfriend to church. I cringed when I heard he was coming but kept my mouth shut, all the while praying that by some miracle of God his hair would grow and change color and his clothes not smell and by the grace of our dear Lord he not wear his combat boots.

Sabbath morning came and one out of three miracles came to life — the clothes, even though they were the same clothes he always wore, did not smell. The hair and combat boots came too. And of all church mornings to be attending a sister church across town, much smaller than our campus church sanctuary where we could halfway hide…

To top it off, we were late arriving thanks to having to wait on our beloved guest. Thus, we were given the honor of being ushered in at the first pause in the service… all the way down to the front of the church. Yep, we were on the front row! Bob Uecker would have been proud.

It was like the old E. F. Hutton commercial. Everyone, and I do mean **everyone** in the church sanctuary stopped and looked… and looked, and continued to stare in utter amazement as we paraded down the aisle to our seats, his combat boots glistening from an apparent early morning shine. One woman sitting across from us never stopped looking throughout the entire service!

Several minutes further into the service, the time came for visitors to be greeted. Thank goodness the pastor hustled over to us and warmly greeted all of us. He was genuine, as if to be saying to this wild look-ing boy, "You're truly welcome here as long as I am the minister." I admired him for that. I found out later that Pastor Halverson had seen it all in his many years of service to the Lord, including having worked with kids and addicts on the streets of New York City years ago. He's a dynamic preacher… By sermon's end and closing I was prepared to again face the masses. I finally left there in one piece.

Shannon knew how to shock me. I'll never forget the experience as long as I live… the look on those people's faces as we walked down the aisle.

Little did Shannon know, however, that the incident was to be of great significance to me. I learned a great deal about myself that day. It was the beginning of my shedding the "what will people think" mentality. Oh, it would stay with me for many months to come. After all, I had it ingrained in me for a number of years. However, I saw Pastor Halverson's sincerity and genuine concern for all of us. He saw us, especially the kids, from his heart. He knew that my stepdaughter and this boy were crying out for acceptance, not simply defying the norm. He heard their cries that Sabbath morning. I didn't. I was too wrapped up in what people would think of me and my parenting skills. True love of another human spirit becomes blind to the house — the exterior that we all put up to hide behind.

I will admit this. The boy would never start on my team, but I did admire the courage both he and Shannon displayed every time they ventured into mainstream America.

One troubling note from our front row experience... Jamie got lost in the shuffle again. All eyes, all anxieties via Donna and I were focused on her older sister. We must be careful not to let Jamie slip between the cracks on us.

Prayer: Father, why are we so quick to judge others by their outward apearance as opposed to their innermost beliefs and dreams?

Teach me to look at another's eyes, not clothes for understanding.

If there is hurt, help me to see it and comfort their pain.

If there is confusion, guide me to direct them to You without turning them away.

If there is sadness, allow me the opportunity to help them find some measure of joy in their lives.

Teach me to look for Your Son's eyes in others... to look for the eyes of Jesus.

And thank you Heavenly Father for seeing the humor in the hair color of men and boys. It just so happens that Shannon's boyfriend liked red and I prefer Just For Men.

Day # 31 If The Season Ended Today...

The first month of this long season has come to a close. If the season ended today and awards were given out, it would probably go something like this:

Best Offensive Player: Donna, the biological mother. She is explosive!

Best Defensive Player: Jamie, our 14-year-old. She can take the best of what we all dish out, and it doesn't seem to affect her... yet.

She definitely sacrifices herself for the good of the team.

Cy Young Winner (best pitcher): unanimously voted to Shannon, our 16-year-old, hands down. She has more pitches and can change speeds and directions better than anyone I've ever seen. You go up to bat against her, and you leave shaking your head. You're not really sure what pitches she threw at you — you just know that by the end of the day you're 0 for 4 with two strikeouts.

Most Valuable Player: Kendra, the tiny, throwaway dog that everyone loves to hate. No matter how much you fuss at her, throw her off the couch... she just keeps coming back for more. She even got semi-run over by a car the other day and it didn't seem to phase her. If anything, she seems calmer now.

Coach of the Year: No one really knows, to date, who the coach is. Donna thinks I'm calling the shots. The kids think they're calling the shots. I still jump whenever Chelsey barks and heads for the basement.

Thought for the Day: Stepfathers are not born. They are molded... and molded until one day they have the "right stuff" to take over as head coach... head of the household. For a select few, it only takes a few months. For others it may take years. Still others may never grab hold of that brass ring.

A word to the wise few who think the brass ring is out of reach... Get help now! Otherwise, you'll be eaten alive! Stepparenting is no place for losers. Kids' lives are at stake here. If you're having trouble getting with the program now, imagine where you will be in six months if you don't get help.

Learn to talk to your partner... your wife about your fears and anxieties. Shoot straight with each other for the sake of the children and your marriage.

Find a trusted buddy (I said Buddy— not another female!) to talk to, especially if he, too, is a father of the biological kind or better yet, stepfather like you.

Find a support group in your community or church.

Stay close to God. In the end, your relationship with Him and Jesus is all that will pull you through.

Don't forget to laugh at yourself.

And by all means, know some measure of joy in each day of your life too.

Remember the Creed…

I am a stepfather. I was born to be a father. Regardless of my past path, I can be a positive role model to my children… I, too, was re-created by God in His own image and do possess the God-given capabilities to serve my wife faithfully and honestly. I can faithfully serve my new family with dignity and honor… I **am** one of the new breed…

───────────────

The most important thing a father can do for his
children is to love their mother.
Theodore Hesburgh

"I love family meetings."

5

the party's over

coach: 1. hired to a lifetime contract, but the biological head coach may show up at any time to disrupt the team. **2.** your wages are garnished every month. **3.** your players have a strong union, who advocate monthly allowance increases and frequent srikes if demands are not met. **4.** your opponent changes rapidly, and you never have a homecourt advantage because you're never sure where your home field is.

ref-er-ee: 1. mother. **2.** biologically in control of the game and will always pull a power play — call a technical foul — if the players and/ or the coach are "losing it". **3.** changes the rules of the game in midstream to accomodate all. **4.** uncanny ability to allow both the players and the coach to "dump on her". **5.** understands the players and their games far better than the coach, and understands what it's like to wear the coach's hat. **6.** looks good in stripes…

Day # 37 Let's Go To Work…

We're at that point in the season when the kinks should have been worked out, the starting line-ups and rotations set, and the team has settled in to find that "groove."

About the only groove I've found is the railing next to the bed at night after the house has finally settled in and the stadium lights have been turned off. Unfortunately, it's usually after midnight before the phone stops ringing, the dogs stop barking… the sirens outside cease.

I'm beginning to understand the magnitude of what I've taken on here. However, I can't think about it too much or I run the risk of losing a positive outlook. These kids need so much and demand so much attention; if not physical, there's an ever-increasing emotional strain on me, worrying and wondering… "Am I doing the right thing? Should I back off this or that?"

It's easy to say that all these kids need is someone to love them and… that's true. They need unconditional love and acceptance from me, especially from me. Their past history with the adult male species has not been a positive one, and that's being kind to their biological father.

Unconditional love and acceptance… how do you develop that in an environment where chaos and strife appear to be the rule rather than the exception? I worked with teenage girls before, and I don't remember… That's it though. I worked with them. I did not live with them. I did not accept the responsibility of fatherhood with them twenty-four hours a day, seven days a week, night after day after night.

And what about my relationship with Donna? It's hard enough adjusting to a new bride, much less a new family. Donna is good for me, and I know deep in my heart that God put me with her for a reason. Surely the Almighty One was not that put out with me — I mean I made my share of mistakes and… No, there's a reason that He has not shared with me yet. In His own time when He thinks I'm ready, He will tell me.

In the mean time, I just have to hang tough and keep my heart open to Him. And continue to pray that the two beasts (dogs, not girls, although at times…) go out the back door one day and never come back.

> *Thought for the Day: It is not the critic who counts, not the man who points out how the strong man stumbles or where the doer of deeds could have done them better. The credit belongs to the man who is actually in the arena, whose face is marred by dust and sweat and blood, who strives valiantly, who errs and comes up short again and again because there is no effort without error and shortcomings, who knows the great devotion, who spends himself in a worthy cause, who at best knows in the end the high achievement of triumph and at worst, if he fails while daring greatly, knows his place shall never be with those timid and cold souls who know neither victory or defeat.*
>
> *Theodore Roosevelt*

Day # 39 Dog Gone Madness…

Don't **ever** wish that your dog leaves you. He, or in this case, she will pay you back.

Our large beast, Chelsey, has a fondness for cats. She likes to eat them. I don't think the Good Lord intended for hunting trips to occur on Sabbath mornings. We were getting ready for church, and Chelsey approached me and barked. In Chelsey language, that means let me out and fast or I'll leave you something to remember me by in the basement… that's what it means to me anyway since I somehow inherited basement duty… although I should not have been surprised, given that I'm the only male in the house and women are born with this notion that men and basement duty go hand-in-hand — in Chelsey's case, hand and shovel…

The Party's Over

As I was saying, being the good-hearted father that I was, not to mention responsible beast owner, I let Chelsey out without looking into our back yard. Within seconds I heard screeches and screams that would have scared even the scariest soul. About that time it seemed everyone in the house and probably the neighborhood looked out into the yard and saw our beast with her victim in her mouth. By the time I got there the stray cat was dead... stiff as a board.

Chelsey approached me seeking some type of sick approval. I approached the women in my life seeking some type of sick advice. I was handed a garbage bag and a broom.

Need I say more?

I must say fatherhood has its moments...

Prayer: Dear Father, Maker of all things, if it's true cats have nine lives, please allow this stray another life away from the beast that I now own.

And Father, forgive me for slinging him in the dumpster up the road. I knew not what else to do...

And as for the beast — give me some ideas on behavior management with dogs. Needless to say, an extended time-out in the basement will only punish me in the end...

Father, I know all life is precious and sacred, but do You and Your angels fall out of Your heavenly seats laughing when you see us humans doing crazy things?

You grow up the day you have the
first real laugh — at yourself.
Ethel Barrymore

Day # 44 Family Starting Rotation…

Well, I've lived through the cycle now and I know what to expect from here on out. **Can somebody please get me out of here?**

The month starts with Jamie, my youngest. She probably fits your textbook definition of "girl on…" She gets moody and somewhat depressed. She throws a tantrum or two and you wonder why she's so upset at something so trivial until you realize — Hey, it's Jamie's time. Within a few days Jamie is back to her happy-go-lucky, normal self.

Next up is Donna… Well, let's just say that for one ten-to-twelve hour span of time every month, two plus two does not equal four. And why should it anyway, unless of course you were guilty of doing something wrong… And just what did you do today? I don't believe you, even though I know you were where you were suppose to be — I was there too! And I still don't understand… You get the message? I mean it's as if a psychotic break wandered through the house and latched on to her like a virus or something. Then, poof… it's gone, and she's left wondering why I'm lying with the dogs with our heads buried underneath the blanket in the basement!

Third up for our "usual" monthly rendezvous with womanhood is Shannon, our lovely 16-year-old. Actually, I'm not always positive when Shannon's time has arrived because she seems manic/depressive to me all the time. Yet, the people I've talked to with older teenage girls say it's normal and not to worry about it. If that is normal, I want off the planet now!

Last, but certainly not least… me. I finally called a family meeting the other night — you know, when everybody actually sits down at the table for more than five minutes at a time. I asked the women in my life if I, too, could have a rotation in the cycle. "No problem," they said. "Just tell us when you're due since you act like you're on…. about three-fourths of the time anyway." I love family meetings…

Anyway, I'm in the rotation now. Quite a starting rotation we have too… as tough as there is in any league.

Day # 53 Blessed be the Day…

Hey, one of those days you write home about… when you hit for the cycle — forget Day # 44… I'm talking about every ballplayers' dream day… a single, double, triple, and home run in one game!

We had a wonderful family outing after church today. We went to a park for a picnic, strolled along the trails laughing, played on the swings and monkey bars. I watched Donna interact with her daughters today and saw a bond there that I can only imagine what it must feel like. There is a love there that knows no bounds. I see that and then I try to imagine the love that Jesus felt for His people… feels for us now, along with the love that God shares with all of us if we simply fall on our knees and ask for it. If that doesn't put a warm glow throughout your body…

I still cannot imagine what it must feel like to carry a child for nine months and give birth… We're talking emotional stuff here, not the physical act of conceiving. My wife has already assured me that my quarterly bouts with hemorrhoids do not qualify. If that's the case, count me out because I cannot even begin to imagine…

Back to the emotional stuff… to carry and conceive a child, and then to proceed to raise that "little me" from birth through childhood… to adolescence, and finally adulthood. I wish I could **feel** that bond that Donna feels with her kids.

I sometimes wish that I could feel that bond that any halfway decent male should feel towards his biological children. I've never had kids, and Donna and I have no plans to start now. I've never felt a need to have my genes and my namesake carried onward through history. However, I've often wondered what it must feel like to have a biological child of my own.

I'll never forget my brothers telling me that they would die for their kids in a heartbeat. Donna has told me the same thing on numerous occasions. That's a strong love, an unbreakable bond. I try to imagine loving another human being that much… I guess that is the epitome of unconditional love — the willingness to sacrifice your life for another.

Prayer: Thanks Father for giving me days like today… to see and feel the joy and love that a family can bring.

Thanks for fathers and mothers who truly love their kids unconditionally.

Teach me how to love that way.

Thanks for loving me unconditionally, and for sacrificing Your only begotton Son for me.

Teach me how to love that way.

Thanks for having provided me with earthly parents who loved me unconditionally and taught me about You and Jesus.

Teach me how to lead my children to You.

Teach me how to love that way.

Day # 64 Who's on First?

The past two weeks has been anything but weird, to say the least. It seems I've gone from the penthouse to the outhouse. I've gone from being called "dad" to Joe… to "that man". We've had our normal bumps and bruises (emotional only!) over the past fourteen days, but nothing so paramount to warrant my name change.

Donna must know what's going on. She senses everything when it comes to her kids' feelings. Yet, she's not talking much either. What is everybody afraid of in this house? Am I that difficult to live with? I know I get a little strange at times, but I don't line up my shoes anymore. I'm learning how to live with dishes left in the sink, laundry left in the dryer (and yes, I'm still averaging one pair of underwear and three mateless socks/week behind that clothes-devouring dryer). Granted, I still have a difficult time with the thermostat moving from 60 to 80 degrees half-a-dozen times in the course of a so-called normal day. And I did go semi-ballistic over a $300 phone bill. And I'm moody and withdrawn at times. I don't do a very good job of telling my family how I feel. I'm great at work… the consumate professional, straight up with people for better or worse for the the sake of the program. However, when it comes to my family and discussing my feelings, I clam up, shut down, hold it all in until… But that's still not the reason everybody has been giving me the silent treatment lately.

Something is going on. I know the girls' biological father called recently. He hasn't had much to do with them over the years. Perhaps the girls are upset that he called, or upset that he left them… or upset that I'm in the picture?

Somebody tell me what's going on around here. Why am I the odd man out all of a sudden? I'm paying the bills, buying the make-up, not him. He hasn't done a thing in years to help, and all of a sudden he calls and he's "dad"… I'm Joe. That's not fair.

Prayer: Father, I'm in over my head here. Open my eyes to what is going on around me with my kids and my wife. Why is it they seem to be pushing me aside? I know I'm trying to be the best stepfather… No! The best father that I can be to those two girls. Why are they rejecting me now? Don't they understand that I have feelings too?

O Lord, please open my eyes. Show me the way.

I'm weary…

Do not pray for easy lives. Pray to be strong men.
Do not pray for tasks equal to your powers but for powers equal to your tasks.
Then the doing of your work will be no miracle, but you will be a miracle.
Every day you shall wonder at the richness of your life which has come to you by the grace of God.
Phillips Brooks

Day # 67 Substitution...

Dear Joe,

Mom said you were upset cause we hadn't been talking to you. It's no big deal. We just get confused when our real dad calls. We never know when he is going to call. He just does every now and then. He tells us that he's our father and that he loves us and wants us to come and see him.

We just don't know what to do. Mom says he hasn't changed much. We don't really know him. We would like to get to know him but don't know how, and we don't want to hurt your feelings either. You've been good to us and good for mom. Believe us... we needed you a long time ago!

Stay cool and we love ya!
Shannon & Jamie

Thought for the Day: I guess that's why we're called **step**fathers. We're not the first step or biological old man. We're the next step. We play second fiddle... back-up quarterback... relief pitcher to the supposed ace of the staff.

Yea, it hurts a bit, but I'm beginning to understand my role. I will never be their biological father, but I'll bet it won't be long before they're calling me "dad" again. They deserve a father who loves them and will go to bat for them. It's too bad their father did not fill those shoes; I'll be glad to step in and give it my best shot. In the end the kids and the Good Lord will know who fought for them.

I may never understand the bond that evolves between a father and his daughter. I'll never feel it like a biological father who had "done it right" would feel it... from watching his little girl grow up before his eyes to the first day of school... to high school and the proms to walking her down that aisle... I may get to experience a few of them, but I can never fully appreciate the moments like the old man... what a joy that must be.

That's okay. It's still a great thrill to see that gleam in their eyes when things are going well. I've been in my business too long and have seen too many damaged family relationships, shattered by neglect, violence, and other forms of abuse. I still cannot fathom how any father could hurt his little girl. What a travesty of life, and yet, it's happening more and more in our society.

I cannot change my status with these two girls that I so proudly and sometimes fearfully call my daughters. I can sure sleep at night, however, knowing that I can be a good stepdad to them. And I can be an example of God's unconditional love to them. And hopefully, I can direct them down the path of kindness and compassion for all.

Prayer: Thanks, Father for giving me the opportunity to experience fatherhood… parenthood, even if it's not of the biological kind. Every responsible and caring adult should have such an opportunity at least once in their lives. There are enough suffering kids out there who need it.

Teach me to listen to the girls' hearts… to intuitively read their every cry for understanding; to not be afraid to show them that I can love them and be there for them, even though I'm not their biological father.

Above all, let them know, Father, that they can get close to me… I will not leave them.

Nothing is so strong as gentleness,
Nothing so gentle as real strength.
St. Francis de Sales

Day # 71 Normal is Dull...

Everything is back to normal around here. One of my favorite music tapes, one that had twenty years of old James Taylor and Carole King, has been upgraded to Guns & Roses... So much for musical memories.

I rarely listen to my stereo anymore. Things that used to be important to me have fallen by the wayside as time marches on and family living materializes. The material things just don't seem to matter that much anymore. Actually, it wouldn't matter if they did because many of them are gone... vanished into thin air or taped over via Nine Inch Nails — now that's a musical group for you.

It's amazing that homework assignments that used to take me a few hours are done in twenty minutes with the stereo on, the TV on, and the phone glued to their ears. Multi-talented these kids of today, able to filter out background noises while they study. Amazing!

Driving lessons have advanced to real roads with real cars and real people. It's **real** scary! We were driving back from a weekend trip recently, and I decided to let Shannon drive on the interstate. What a joy... When her mother had reached the point of almost passing out in the back seat, I told Shannon to take the next exit and pull over somewhere, anywhere. She took the next exit okay, but when she asked, "Where do I pull over?" and I replied, "Right here," well, we proceeded to complete a ninety degree turn into McDonalds at 45 miles per hour! Oh what fun it is to ride...

And about Jamie's amazing ability to drive a 5-speed? Well, it seems my dear, sweet Jamie was taking the Subaru for daily joy rides around the neighborhood before we got home from work. Yes, that's right! I've got a 14-year-old car thief on my hands! And of course, Shannon was completely innocent... only riding in the car every day to protect her younger sister.

We visited our local juvenile detention center the night we found out... Nice place to visit, but I don't think the girls wanted to live there.

Prayer: Lord, You promised me that you would open my eyes and show me the path... Father, I see the light. It looks like a train coming the other way.

Day # 90 Quarterly Report...

Three months into the season and I'm still alive! We're one-fourth of the way through our inaugural season and the dust has yet to settle. Some say it takes several years for the dust to settle in stepfamilies.

I don't have several years at this pace. I feel like I've aged ten years in the past three months. I may need to consider going on the disabled list. A trade however, is out of the question! I'm having too much fun...

And Jesus said unto them, "... If ye have faith as a grain of mustard seed, ye shall say unto this mountain, Remove hence to yonder place; and it shall remove; and nothing shall be impossible unto you."
Matthew 17:20

Never let your head hang low. Never give up and sit down and grieve. Find another way. And don't pray when it rains if you don't pray when the sun shines.
Sachel Paige

"Who's on first? What's on second!"

settling in

au-tumn: 1. The season… fall, when the boys of summer play for all the marbles in the World Series. **2.** fall… football feeding frenzy, gridiron glory all weekend long including Hank and his roudy friends on Monday night… Where is TVbutt? What do you mean the dog chewed them and they don't work? And why is that mutt refusing to get out of my recliner? We're watching what on Monday night?

teen dating: 1. Boy shows up… actually, you can hear the bass from the 6-foot speakers mounted to his car three blocks away. **2.** He has no hair…oops! he turned his head. He's got hair on that side… to go with the five earrings in his ear. You want him to come to the door, but you don't want your neighbors to see him. **3.** Too late, your daughter has already bolted from the house…"Bye mom and dad, love you… I won't be late." Her mother can't bear to look, although her daughter and the speciman sitting in the driver's seat are sitting so low to the ground you couldn't see them anyway.

Day # 101 Crimson and Orange…

Fall is arriving, one of my favorite times of the year when the trees turn to glorious golds and bright reds… when the late September winds blow and the smell of football is in the air.

Football doesn't mean much to my new family. Jamie seems to understand the terminology a little better than her older sister and her mom. She does know the difference between a touchdown and a field goal, although we're pushing it to go into any greater detail of America's love affair with the "controlled" violence game known as football.

Of course, college football is virtually unknown to my new family. None of them could appreciate my witnessing Tennessee football history some thirty years ago when as a bright-eyed, ten-year-old my dad took me to Neyland Stadium. Tennessee was so soundly whipping their opponent that midway through the third quarter they did the unthinkable — Tennessee broke from the single-wing formation and ran a series of plays from the straight T-formation. My dad turned to me and said, "Son, you're witnessing history today." I'll never forget his words on that sun-drenched Autumn afternoon… the smell of popcorn, the huge crowd, the time spent with my dad… just the two of us.

Now my Saturdays are like Sundays used to be as a kid. We attend church on Saturday morning… the Sabbath, and spend the afternoons relaxing at home or in the great outdoors as much as possible… No TV, no shopping, no Tennessee football, at least not "live" unless it's after sundown.

At first, I resented such an abrupt change in my life. However, I could not argue with God's fourth commandment, the real, uncut, uncensored version as stated in Exodus 20: 8-11, not the chopped up version our religious forefathers adopted.

What a novel idea, huh? An entire day set aside for worship and relaxation among family and loved ones. How many families could last an entire day without the TV and a trip to the mall?

I should not have been surprised that the kids looked forward to the Sabbath dinner and picnics. They were disappointed when Donna and I became spiritually lazy on occasion and missed going to church or doing something as a family outdoors.

Can you imagine if our society started honoring the Sabbath as it was intended by our Creator? For me, I'm not too hung up on which day is honored. Having grown up in a Lutheran church, I was accustomed to church on Sunday mornings and the voice of Dizzy Dean and Pee Wee Reese in the early afternoon while the family ate dinner and watched the Yankees or the Cardinals play. I know Seventh-Day Adventists, Baptists, and others who would beg to differ regarding the Sabbath. That's okay. The point to me is families spending time together in worship and relaxation without a bunch of real world distractions.

No, I would not classify any sporting event as an absolute necessity, although the third Saturday in October (Tennessee vs Alabama) might come close.

I've come a long way spiritually in the past six months. I still have a long way to go, especially with unconditional love.

Prayer: O Father, Creator of all great things, continue me on my path of enlightenment and understanding. Help me to keep a healthy perspective on what is truly valuable in my life and what You have told us is important in Your Word and teachings to us.

Thanks for creating us and allowing us to invent a wide variety of sports and recreational activities to play and to watch. We can learn a great deal about ourselves from such activities and events. However, help us to keep a healthy perspective on such and to always keep You and Your commandments first in our hearts.

And Father, regarding that third Saturday in October, keep the Bear in line up there.

Day # 111 One Day at a Time...

Here I am four months into this new life and it just dawned on me — I'm married! It's so easy to get caught up in the day-to-day challenges of fatherhood that I lose sight of my new bride. She's the reason I'm in this mess to begin with!

We sure bring our baggage along from past lives lost when we re-marry. Some of us pack larger bags than others. Some of our luggage is quite old.

My parents were mighty good to me growing up. I never truly realized just how good they were until I became a stepparent. It did not matter how tired, how broke, how sick of kid stuff they might have been... My parents made sure that I was number one in their lives. They were incredibly unselfish as I look back on my childhood days.

So why am I so selfish to my stepkids? Why do I get so bent-out-of-shape over little things like $400 electric bills and $300 phone bills? See, here I go again, focusing on the kids and their maladaptive, loud, boisterous... excuse me, my new bride is getting lost in the shuffle again.

Thought for the Day: Love is a many splendid thing, but living it among two teenage stepdaughters and a wife... and yes, two female dogs, ain't easy. There's an old saying... If you believe it, you gotta live it.

I believe in unselfish parenting. I believe in an unselfish partner-ship with my wife.

I believe that the only way to live it is one day at a time.

That's the best I can do...

That's the best any of us can do.

One day at a time... spirit-filled and childlike.

Faith of a child... Be still and know.

Wisdom is often times nearer when
we stoop than when we soar.
Wordsworth

Day # 122 The Brady Bunch...

Whoever created the Brady Bunch must have been one sick human being. What a standard for our society to live up to, given that every day in this country approximately 1300 new stepfamilies are created. Can you imagine? 1300 every day, day after day... Almost half the marriages on any given day are second time around adventures, many of which include children of divorce. Between joint custody, joint adventures, and joints possibly being inhaled by your teenager, what's a stepparent to do?

I'm lucky. I had no children from my first marriage of five years. Wise choice looking back, although I'll never know the joy of creating and watching a "little me" grow up. My wife has no desire for another child, and frankly, I don't either. We're too old and worn out at this stage of our lives to start another family.

I sometimes try to imagine life if I did have kids from my first marriage. I cannot fathom having custody of my children and my stepchildren all under one roof. Yet, two families are joined as one hundreds of times a day in our society.

Actually, the kids often times experience three families rolled into one by the time all is said and done. Initially, they must endure the demise of their nuclear family, then learn to live in a single-parent home, often times with joint custody, and then be joined together in holy matrimony with a stepparent... perhaps even stepsiblings, not to mention another set of in-laws... The possibilities become endless. To top it off, there may be visitation to the "lost" biological parent, who may or may not even keep up with his/her kids after the divorce. Hardly seems fair, or normal for that matter.

The sad part is divorce is here to stay. We're too far gone in our instant gratification, quick fix, no commitment lifestyles to significantly turn the tide on our high divorce rate. Maybe that would be an easier pill to swallow if kids were not thrown into the middle of the entire mess, not to mention played off as pawns by emotionally scarred parents. Without a strong spiritual base, many stepfamilies are doomed to repeat the past.

Meanwhile, lucky me... another day gone by and I can't find any socks to match for tomorrow, the dog has my underwear in her mouth, and Sears is calling wondering why our payment is late. Oh, and did I mention... our devious, underwear-devouring dryer is at it again... chewed up and spit out my one and only pair of Jim Palmer Jockey's. I tell you, I just don't get any respect around here...

Thought for the Day: Be not deceived; God is not mocked: for whatsoever a man soweth that shall he also reap. For he that soweth to his flesh shall of the flesh reap corruption; but he that soweth to the spirit shall of the spirit reap everlasting.
Galatians 6: 7,8

Day # 135 Rituals...

Tuesday night... time to get all the garbage out to the trash for Wednesday's pickup. Why is it no one else in this house is aware of when the garbage is due? It just doesn't seem important to them.

Me? I always remember that the garbage trucks run on Wednesdays and the recycle trucks run on Mondays — the recycle bin must be carried to the front yard either on Sunday nights or Monday mornings as we leave for work. So why am I running around the house on Sunday nights picking up all the empty shampoo bottles, Wisk bottles, and coke cans, not to mention half-emptied soup cans thrown in the trash? And why is it after five months of preaching, the kids still throw their empty cans in the garbage as opposed to taking the additional eight steps to toss them in the bin on the back porch? I have even left coke cans on the kitchen table to see if anyone would toss them in the bin. Nope… they just sit there for at least twelve hours, and that's far too long for any stray can to sit unattended on a table. Why is it unattended items are so insignificant in this house? Am I that strange or what?

P. S. TVbutt was left on the couch last night as opposed to being placed on the shelf. Can you imagine that?

Prayer: Father, I know I'm obsessive/compulsive about orderliness… am I that out of line around here? Why did You put me with such a disorganized bunch? Is there a lesson in life You're trying to teach me?

Open my eyes to the message, please… and soon. The newspapers are piling up and we have run out of those thin, garbage bag ties that twist neatly six times.

Day # 142 Feelings…

I guess I've been so wrapped up in my own self-pity that I failed to see what my new family has to deal with when it comes to me. I do border on insanity when it comes to neatness and orderliness. When I complete my weekly vacuuming… moving furniture not included, and quarterly mopping routine, I don't understand why objects need to be moved again once they are back in place. Is it wrong to want everything put up or put away all the time, regardless of circumstances? If I am honest with myself, the answer is overwhelmingly yes!

It is sad to admit, but I have seen fear in my girls' eyes when I came home from work and found things in disarray. I hate that. The girls know I'm a nonviolent person and would never strike them for any reason. Yet, what I do is not much better — I clam up. I give them the silent treatment. They walk through the living room and I don't even acknowledge their existence.

My kids and my new bride have taught me some downright ugly things about myself, one of which is I truly don't know how to express my anger. I usually give them the silent treatment until the afternoon comes that I "blow a fuse" — I verbally chew them up and spit them out. I hurt them, and I truly don't mean to. It's just days or weeks of anger spewing like an exploding coke bottle.

I'm working on learning to express my anger in a more appropriate and timely fashion… like when it happens. I chastise my wife for bringing up two-week-old incidents, yet I'm doing no better by holding it all in and then blowing up over something trivial and unrelated. It's messy dealing with feelings that way. There is no real winner.

Thought for the Day: It is not what we see and touch or that which others do for us which makes us happy; it is that which we think and feel and do, first for the other fellow and then for ourselves.
Helen Keller

Prayer: O Great Spirit, whose breath gives life to the world, and whose voice is heard in the soft breeze;
We need your strength and wisdom.
Cause us to ever walk in beauty. Give us eyes ever to behold the red and purple sunset.
Make us wise so that we may understand what you have taught us.
Help us to learn lessons you have hidden in every leaf and rock.
Make us always ready to come to you with clean hands and steady eyes.
So when life fades, like the fading sunset, our spirits may come to you without shame. Amen.
Traditional Native American Prayer

Day # 153 The Dating Game...

My father would roll over in his grave if he could see the likes of the boys that pick up my girls for dates. I've never seen such hairdos... from no hair "wannabees" for my younger daughter to the hippies of the '90's for my oldest. It seems the times they are always a changin, yet some things forever remain the same.

Boys still dread meeting the fathers of the girls. Well, some boys do anyway — the ones who know enough about common courtesy and manners to come to the door. The others have a difficult time getting out of their cars to come to the door... too much of an inconvenience for their egos. Brash is putting it mildly for many of today's youth. After all, Sir Charles (Barkley) is not here to serve as a role model. That's too bad. We sure need them.

Anyway, we're at the five month mark and I'm still kickin! Our team is improving and we have probably turned the corner on this thing called family living.

Time will tell, especially with the dreary, late fall / early winter days approaching, not to mention the challenge of the holidays. They should be interesting...

Thought for the Day: The great thing in this world is not so much where we are, but what direction we are moving.
Oliver Wendell Holmes

Your family is grown up when your kids stop asking you where they came from and refuse to tell you where they're going.
Jacob M. Braude

In Memory of my Father...
(who taught me the value of manners and respect)

... he that giveth, let him do so with simplicity...
Romans 12:8

The young boy entered the diner and sat at the counter as the lunch hour regulars came in and the seats started filling up. A waitress abruptly approached the boy with a glass of water, sensing that more important customers were ready to be served.

"How much for an ice cream sundae?" the boy asked.

"Ninety-nine cents," snapped the waitress.

The boy reached into his pocket, pulled out his change, and started to count... "How 'bout an ice cream cone? How much does that cost?"

The waitress coldly replied, "Seventy- nine cents." She had little time for this child. Her customers were coming in.

The boy again counted his coins, then replied, "I'll have the cone."

The waitress grabbed the boy's money, brought him the ice cream cone and walked away. Several minutes later she passed by his chair and noticed the boy was gone. He had quietly left.

The waitress stood staring at his placemat on the counter. There she found neatly stacked one dime, one nickel, and five pennies... her tip.

Everyone has a choice in life: he may approach it as a creator or a critic, a lover or a hater, a giver or a taker.
Anonymous

"literally gone to the dogs..."

holiday cheer & dreams

vi-sion: 1. unusual wisdom in foreseeing what is going to happen. **2.** the ability to see, smell, taste, feel, and hear a scene in your mind with absolute clarity, knowing that you can create it in due time with the God-given capabilities you have.

foot-prints: 1. the area on a surface covered by something. **2.** "The Lord replied, My precious child, I love you and I would never leave you. During your time of trial and suffering, when you see only one set of footprints, it was then that I carried you."

Day # 164 The Turkey Bowl...

I missed the Turkey Bowl this year, the annual backyard football fiasco at my mom's house on Thanksgiving where my brothers and their kids and I played our own brand of football.

Instead, I saw cow patties, horses, ponies and peacocks... and not a turkey in sight, nor on our plates. We had vegetarian turkey. The dressing was good, but there's something about Thanksgivings past that will always be special... of getting up to catch a glimpse of the big parade on TV to the annual midday feast as we watched the Detroit Lions play, then outside to play our own version of the game... only to return to eat more turkey and settle in as the Cowboys roared down the field in the late afternoon Texas sun.

My new family has no concept of what I'm talking about. Yet, I have to admit I have no concept of ponies and hayrides either on a Thanksgiving day spent horsing around the farm. Perhaps I should feel fortunate to have the opportunity to experience a new way of life... a new way of celebrating an old tradition. After all, there is life after the Turkey Bowl.

Prayer: Father, our families of origin and our stepfamilies are often quite different. Help me to appreciate the differences and to learn from them, never to dwell on good times lost but rather, to dwell on fond memories of Thanksgivings past... and to cherish the opportunity to celebrate Thanksgivings to come in a different way.

Father, a special Thanksgiving prayer to those men like my earthly father, who labored so long just to provide his family with the means to sit down in a warm home with plenty of food and loved ones to enjoy.

Thought for the Day: "The Bag Lady"
 She used to sleep in the Fifth Street Post Office. I could smell her before I rounded the entrance to where she slept, standing up,

by the public phones. I smelled the urine that seeped through the layers of decay from her nearly toothless mouth. If she was not asleep, she mumbled incoherently.

Now they close the post office at six to keep the homeless out, so she curls up on the sidewalk, talking to herself, her mouth flapping open as though unhinged, her smells diminished by the soft breeze.

One Thanksgiving we had so much food left over, I packed it up, excused myself from the others and drove over to Fifth Street.

It was a frigid night. Leaves were swirling around the streets and hardly anyone was out, all but a few of the luckless in some warm home or shelter. But I knew I would find her.

She was dressed as she always was, even in summer: the warm, woolly layers concealing her old, bent body. Her bony hands clutched the precious shopping cart. She was squatting against a wire fence in front of the playground next to the post office. "Why didn't she choose some place more protected from the wind?" I thought, and assumed she was so crazy she did not have the sense to huddle in a doorway.

I pulled my shiny car to the curb, rolled down the window and said, "Mother... would you..." and was shocked at the word "Mother." But she was... is... in some way I cannot grasp.

I said, again, "Mother, I've brought you some food. Would you like some turkey and stuffing and apple pie?"

At this the old woman looked at me and said quite clearly and distinctly, her two lower teeth wobbling as she spoke, "Oh, thank you very much, but I'm quite full now. Why don't you take it to someone who really needs it." Her words were clear, her manners gracious. Then I was dismissed: her head sank into her rags again.

Bobbie Probstein

Day # 167 A Christmas Tree...

The four of us went out and bought a Christmas tree today. The girls and Donna were excited. I was cold! But, I was excited too, and thrilled to see my family's exuberance over an old needle-nozed pine tree. We decorated the tree tonight, flashing lights and all. At times, I still feel like an outsider to these three lovely ladies.

It's obvious watching them around the tree that Christmas is special to them. They have shared so much together over the years. I feel so close to them and yet so far away. Sometimes, I think the girls and Donna are still holding back... still uncertain about my commitment to them... afraid that I will leave them too.

I can only hope and pray that someday they will come to know that I'm in it till the cows come home. They need a man to stick around in their lives, no matter how many cow patties appear on the horizon.

Thought for the Day:
Within every man there is the reflection of a woman, and
Within every woman there is the reflection of a man.
Within every man and woman there is also the reflection
Of an old man and an old woman,
A little boy and a little girl.

Hyemeyohsts Storm

To every thing there is a season, and a time to every
purpose under the heaven.
Ecclesiastes 3:1

Day # 181 If You Build It, They Will Come…

It dawned on me while driving home from work that the number of stepfamily combinations is seemingly endless. You've got those like myself who were married before but had no children; and then there are the never-before-married who venture into "married with children." And then, there are the thousands who join forces every year — divorced men and women, each with kids, who marry and combine families. Some of those scenarios involve full or part-time custody; some involve no custody and no visitation. Some unfortunately involve no visitation and no financial assistance even though child support is mandated. It's good to finally see judges and law authorities taking a stronger stand with "deadbeat" dads and moms. Can you imagine being a child in that situation? Your biological dad or mom has all but thrown you away, and on top of that, your custodial parent remarries into a family of kids. Sound confusing? And we expect the kids to make a smooth transition?

I look at my two stepdaughters, and I'm amazed that they are still in one piece… still functioning. I say that because I'm just now beginning to realize how much even adolescents want and depend upon a father figure to hold onto. As a relative newcomer to the art of parenthood, I've had nothing to base the significance of such a relationship or bond on… no gauge or prior history to fully appreciate what value the kids place on my role.

As a result, an encounter with the kids that seemed trivial to me may have been of great importance to them. How was I to know?

What about stepparents who do have biological children from a previous marriage? Do they also miss the boat with their stepchildren? Are they more sensitive to seemingly trivial interactions?

One thing is becoming very clear in my head — I need a group of stepfathers to talk to… to pick their brains… stepfathers from various scenarios to discuss how we can become better parents, better stepfathers… who knows — perhaps even better husbands.

What if... what if stepfathers from all walks of life were given an opportunity to bond? Yes, good old male bonding, but on a different plane... with no TV, no football, and little or no mention of work.

If you built it would they come? Would grown men of varying degrees, talents, and temperaments let go of their male egos for one night a week to discuss their true feelings? Might one even be so bold as to shed a tear or two? Of course, no one would dare tell of such an event outside of the meeting. Our macho man image could remain in check back in the real world. Bur for one or two glorious hours a week, could the great descendants of Adam bare it all with each other for the betterment of their stepfamilies?

I keep hearing this whisper tonight... "If you build it, they will come."

Prayer: Father in Heaven, is this You whispering in my ear? I think it's You, but I sometimes let my head get in the way. I'm trying to listen with my heart. Help me.

I know there must be thousands of stepfathers out there wondering why they were called upon to fill such a void. It's comforting to know I'm not alone in my journey. But I need help bringing us together. As you know Father, we're not real good at sharing our feelings, especially our vulnerabilities.

Guide me on this journey. If You want it built, give me some kind of sign that they, indeed, will show up. Shed some light...

Thought for the Day: There isn't enough darkness in all the world to snuff out the light of one litle candle..
Anonymous

Day # 189 Christmas Eve...

I had a vision earlier this evening as I lay in bed unable to sleep, filled with anticipation and excitement.

I saw a group of men from all walks of life, young and old, rich and poor, sitting together in a clubhouse discussing their children... their stepchildren.

There were no big screen TV's, no pool tables, no women. Just a group of men candidly talking about the joys and struggles of stepparenting.

A brotherhood of men...

And then there was this voice, "If you build it, they will come."

It didn't sound like Santa to me. It sounded much, much bigger.

Thought for the Day: Sometimes the greatest gifts received are mere thoughts... visions of what can be if the Spirit of God is free to fill one's heart.

Once you begin to trust your heart you will realize than when something brings you joy and fulfillment it is the will of God speaking through your heart.
Emmanuel

It is only by forgetting yourself that you draw near to God.
Thoreau

Day # 190 And Thou Shall Call His Name Jesus...

The kids and Donna awoke very early. Me? I never slept! I was too excited, this being my first Christmas with my wife and stepkids... My family.

Everyone seemed a little tense, unsure as to what to do first. But it didn't take long for the kids to decide who was to play Santa Claus.

Nothing fancy, just straight from the heart. I only wished that I could somehow turn the clock back and make the kids young again. I sensed they had the same wish, too.

Thought for the Day: We adults always say that Christmas is for the kids, and it's true — there's nothing like the exuberance of children on a Christmas morning. There's nothing like the joy parents feel when they see their kids excited over a new toy or bicycle… especially if dad spent half the night trying to figure out how to put it together!

Yet, do we really take the time to think about the true significance of this day we call Christmas? Does anybody ever sing happy birthday to Jesus?

Prayer: Heavenly Father, let us give thanks to You for the many gifts we share with each other… the gifts of love and laughter, of peace and joy, of tall tales and tenderness, of food and friendship and family.

Father, most preciously, let us give thanks to You for the ultimate sacrifice of Your Son, Jesus. As we celebrate his birthday and look ahead to a new year, let us seize the opportunity to share Your Son's love with at least one of the lost sheep. For the time may be near… We know Your Son is returning.

Day # 197 New Year's Day…

A far cry from last year when I was in my new apartment with my new furniture, a new life, and no place to go. Today, I have someone to watch the bowl games with, and yet, I don't recall the TV being on. I think I caught a glimpse of the Orange Bowl. I didn't really care. My, how things change…

I enjoyed a New Year's Day down on the farm with my family. We went to my in-laws for black-eyed peas and wound up spending the day enjoying the fresh air. The more I hang around Donna's dad, the more I understand Donna. Today was just another day to him… a day to feed the animals, spend some quiet time in the woods, and work with his ponies. He's a dawn-to-dusk kinda guy, yet he knows how to relax in the course of a long day.

As we returned to our house tonight, we entered to find Chelsey and Kendra stretched out on what used to be my new couch and loveseat. A year ago it was brand new. Today, it has literally gone to the dogs. I almost felt guilty moving Chelsey off the couch.

A year ago I was so alone. Tonight I've got five females living with me. It sounds crazy but I can't imagine going back to the lonliness. I can still imagine reducing my live-in numbers to three, yet even those two old mutts are starting to grow on me.

If someone had told me a year ago…

Thought for the Day: Just when you think you got life figured out…

Prayer: Father, thanks for making this past year something special. I never dreamed that becoming a stepfather would be part of Your plan for me. I would have been perfectly content with a loving wife like Donna and no kids. But, You have issued a blessing and a challenge under one roof. Give me the strength and courage to live up to Your Son's expectations in the year to come, knowing that if I fall short, Jesus will be there to pick me up… and sometimes carry me onward.

Footprints

One night a man had a dream. He dreamed he was walking along the beach with the Lord. Across the sky flashes scenes from his life. For each scene, he noticed two sets of footprints in the sand; one belonging to him, and the other belonging to the Lord.

When the last scene of his life flashed before him, he looked back at the footprints in the sand. He noticed that many times along the path of his life there was only one set of footprints. He also noticed that it happened at the very lowest and saddest times in his life.

This really bothered him and he questioned the Lord about it. "Lord, you said that once I decided to follow you, you'd walk with me all the way. But I have noticed that during the most troublesome times in my life, there is only one set of footprints. I don't understand why when I needed you the most you would leave me."

The Lord replied, "My precious, precious child, I love you and I would never leave you. During those times of trial and suffering, when you see only one set of footprints, it was then that I carried you."

Author Unknown

"Dear God, when the commode runneth over..."

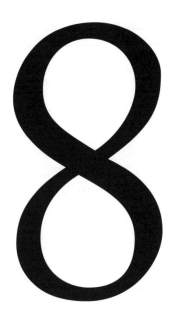

the birth of the
brotherhood

TVbutt: 1. repetitive behavior. **2.** inability to interact socially, characterized by absorption in self-stimulatory behavior. **3.** a small black box, which when activated by the male species, causes severe withdrawal, mute behavior, and extreme anxiety when the wife decides to hide the buttons for the weekend.

Tool Time: 1. Some men were born to be fixers of gadgets, unstoppers of sinks, and jumpstarters of cars. **2.** Some men were born to hit a baseball or throw a football. **3.** Some men were born to paint or sing. **4. All** men were born to push TVbutt. No man was born to sacrifice his aforementioned God-given talent to fix his own house. It goes against man's nature to spend his hard-earned, precious freetime fixing his own stuff… maybe the neighbor's… maybe his best buddy's; never his own. **UNLESS**, of course, it has to do with the greatest of all male talents — watching three football games simultaneously on his big screen TV.

male ego: 1. fragile, easily deflated. **2.** often times too connected to anatomy. **3.** handle with caution… and care.

Day # 213 Shannon's Birthday

My oldest stepdaughter, Shannon, turned seventeen today. My little hippie girl is still as hippyish as ever. But, one thing has changed over the past year that I am proud of. Shannon trusts me. She respects me. She still doesn't do what I ask her to do, but I've gained a measure of respect in her refusals. Actually, she's a good kid simply trying to find her way, as are most seventeen-year-olds.

Frankly, I wouldn't go back to that age in this particular day and time for all the money in the world. I drove to a nearby high school the other morning, and it was like a downtown traffic jam, not to mention the cops and the drug sniffing dogs running around. Times have changed and I want no part of that change.

I had the honor of taking Shannon to see *Les Miserables* at the Tennessee Performing Arts Center for her birthday. She was awe-struck, like a little girl… like her mother — timid and shy around the "who's who" crowd mingling in the lobby at intermission. In fact, I saw a great deal of her mom in Shannon tonight.

I felt like a real father. Seeing Shannon's eyes light up made me glow inside. Sometimes I wish that Donna and I had met when the kids were young. I know my bond with the kids would feel stronger if that had happened. Yet, I'm looking forward to watching the two of them grow into adulthood, knowing that I can be the type of father they always wanted — an easy mark for a few bucks and the car keys!

Thought for the Day: Have you said something positive to your kids today? Tuck them in tonight and tell them how much you love them. And ask them what they are looking forward to tomorrow… In each day, a child should know some joy and have something to look forward to.

Day # 217 Beginnings…

> *The intellect has little to do on the road to discovery.*
> *There comes a leap in consciousness, call it intuition or*
> *what you will, and the solution comes to you and you*
> *don't know how or why.*
> *Albert Einstein*

The light bulb came on inside my head. In fact, it just about blinded me! I love it when the Lord reveals things to me in such an abrupt fashion. I knew that it had to be built.

The flyers were sent out, the word scattered about. It was billed as men's night out… no females allowed, no pets, no discussion of work, all the free food and cola one could muster, and no names required. The only rules? (#1) You had to be a stepfather; and (#2) you had to be willing to check your ego at the door.

Of course, the most sophisticated of scientific instruments was utilized to determine the best night to schedule our inaugural meeting — the TV log. Thursday looked promising. There were no NFL reruns on ESPN, the NBA had a light schedule, no home town action on tap, and it was safe to assume that most men had grown sick of Roseanne. After all, she had butchered the national anthem in front of a packed house at Busch Stadium, not to mention grabbing her — well, in case you missed it, she forever destroyed her goods with any red-blooded American male who clearly understands the concept of groping and spitting.

The date was set. The clubhouse was given a fresh coat of paint. Crackerjacks and cokes were on their way. Only one question remained — would they come?

Thought for the Day: Faith and fear… one is a five-letter word filled with joy and serene anticipation; the other is a four headed monster telling you how foolish you are to even think that such a crazy idea would materialize.

When faith and fear start playing ping pong in my head, it's the closest I ever come to a true psychotic break. My rational mind keeps telling me that it won't work; I'll be embarrassed. It will destroy what little self-esteem I must have to even think that... Then, I let go of my rational mind and listen to my heart. I feel the warmth, the glow... I sense the presence of God, telling me to be still. I see the meeting with undefiled clarity... men opening up to each other, talking about what turns out to be their most important role on this earth — parenting.

I know that God gave me... gave us all the power to create. He made us in His likeness.

Day # 222 January 26th... Our First Date Anniversary

One year ago to the day, my life forever changed thanks to an attractive, blonde RN named Donna. Hard to believe it has only been a year since our first date. It seems like ten!

Prayer: Thanks, heavenly Father, for giving me a second chance. I know You frown upon failed marriages just as You do with all sin. I also know, however, that forgiveness is ours for the asking thanks to the ultimate sacrifice of Your Son, Jesus, for our sins. Father, continue to bless our relationship as we move forward. It is so easy to get caught up in the day-to-day trappings of family responsibility that a couple can lose sight of each other. Give us the hindsight to learn and grow, the foresight to steer the course and enjoy each other along the way, and the vision to see the kids one day successfully on their own so that Donna and I can retreat to the beach.

Day # 232 Men of Courage…

6:35 P.M. The clubhouse is ready, the cola is on ice; the popcorn and crackerjacks on the counter, hardback chairs arranged in a circle. No, change that to rows. No, that's too impersonal; make it a… No! that's too intimidating. Just leave the chairs scattered and see what transpires.

7:05 P.M. Thirty minutes from kickoff; no early arrivals thus far. I guess warmups are out of the question tonight.

7:30 P.M. Five minutes to showtime and no one has… Wait a minute! Yes! It's a man! He's coming my way. He's in! We have made contact.

7:40 P.M. Our inaugural meeting of Stepfathers' Anonymous is under way. Two brave men and me…

John is a 27-year-old accountant who looks the part. He's getting married for the second time in a few weeks to a woman who has two young boys, ages three and five. John had no children from his first marriage of three years. It seems while John was busy crunching numbers, his wife was busy seeing another man. She eventually ran off with him, leaving John crushed. (By the way, John is not an official stepfather yet, but we waived the rule anyway.) He came tonight because he is scared to death of marrying again and losing another woman; and he's also not sure her boys will like him. In fact, John thinks they pretty much hate his guts.

Paul is a 41-year-old construction worker who recently married and inherited a 12-year-old stepdaughter. Paul has two teenage boys, ages fourteen and eleven, from a previous marriage. He has custody of his boys two weekends/month and on designated holidays. According to Paul, his house is on the verge of exploding. His wife told him to get his… over to this meeting and learn something fast! Paul's not shy. He is scared however.

I was amazed. For almost two hours we simply talked. We shared our concerns about our families, our fears, and our anger. There was no need for a "let's do a group warm-up exercise to put everyone at ease…" The three of us, all from different backgrounds and professions, immediately started talking. Grown men opening up so early in the game. Who would have thought?

After it was over, as I turned out the clubhouse lights and headed home, I realized that we had just participated in something very unique. There was no spirit of competition among the participants… no "one upsmanship" at play. Almost immediately, everyone sensed their family dynamic was unique, and there was no need to compete for who had it the toughest or who was the best stepfather. The overriding factor was simple — each of us has our hands full, and can anyone shed some light on how we can keep our roofs from blowing off. After all, we're all stepfathers here.

Granted, it was only a group of three. But, if three can do it…

Next week, we'll see.

Prayer: Thanks, Father, for letting them come. As usual, You delivered the goods on time. I never knew noncompetitive male bonding could prove so beneficial and thought provoking… and downright enjoyable. Above all, I felt such a sense of brotherhood among strangers. I learned from these men, these brothers of mine tonight. I also felt their pain and anguish… their genuine desire to become better stepfathers.

Father, keep the brotherhood alive…

For as many as are led by the spirit of God,
they are the sons of God.
Romans 8:10

Day # 241 Tool Time…

The concept of gentle does not exist in our household. The girls, my wife, even the dogs know only one way — rough! Cabinet doors, dresser drawers, slamming doors, slinging dishes… You name it. If it ain't tough it won't last in our house.

No problem, you say. Just fix it, repair it… whatever it takes, just do it! Unfortunately, the concept of "tool time" does not exist in my repertoire. In fact, the notion of a tool box is foreign to my way of thinking. After all, if something goes wrong just call the landlord, right? Someone forgot to tell me when you own a house you are the landlord.

Donna is actually the landlord in our house. Her mind is far more mechanical than mine. All those years of hanging around her father as he fixed anything and everything certainly paid off. On the other hand, all my years of playing ball are of no help when it comes time to fixing the leaky faucets.

It's funny how we often fall into the same patterns that our parents followed. I vividly recall my dad calling the next door neighbor to come and fix whatever went wrong at our house. On the other hand, Donna's dad fixed everything, including some things that a real plumber or electrician should have repaired… or replaced! So what happens when Donna and I marry and we purchase an older home?

I'm trying to learn how to tinker with simple household items, yet my fragile psyche cannot handle the presence of Donna looking over my shoulder watching me struggle. I blow up, and Donna can't understand how something so simple can cause such high anxiety for me. I try to explain my "baggage" to her… I grew up doing one thing and one thing quite well — I was an athlete. I excelled in sports. It got me a college scholarship. I saw places I never would have seen thanks to baseball. I wouldn't change anything about it except my size and speed. Then, I could have made a substantial living in my younger days playing a boy's game.

The Birth of the Brotherhood

The only problem with such a single-minded focus growing up — I shied away from trying new things as an adolescent and young adult. I grew even more insecure with new experiences in my 20's. If I could not do something well within a short period of time, I wanted no part of it. My self-esteem grew fragile when the hood of a car or a tool box was opened.

In my 30's I finally accepted the fact I would not be employable at the local hardware store. I was okay with finding a friend to fix my car.

Then Donna came along with the opposite mentality — total self-reliance and a tool box to prove it, not to mention teenagers who provided numerous opportunities to practice fixing things.

We're learning to share our worlds… our different perspectives on tool time. It's not easy. We don't like to admit it, but we of the male species have fragile egos. We're born with this notion that only a man… a man's man at that, can climb mountains and mount engine blocks… No problem is too big for someone within the brotherhood of men. That's good in many ways. It also causes serious problems when we do not learn to accept the things we cannot change. I believe that's called wisdom, or at least one aspect of it.

A final note tonight — the girls' bathroom "broke." Donna can't fix this one. It's off limits until we can afford a real plumber. No big deal… just me and three females all trying to get ready at the same time in the morning with one shower, one small sink, and one commode. Life's too short…

Prayer:
Dear God,

When the commode runneth over and the sink stoppeth up; when the shower door breaketh and the dresser drawer stucketh; when the oil light lighteth and the lawn mower explodeth, grant me the serenity to let my wife fix it, the courage to take orders from her, and the wisdom to know when to leave well enough alone.

Day # 246 The Hood is Alive...

*When you become willing to hide nothing, you will not
only be willing to enter into communion but will also
understand peace and joy.*
Anonymous

There is nothing like word of mouth advertising... still the best means of promoting a good product. Our encore edition of Stepfathers' Anonymous has grown to nine brave men. John and Paul have returned along with six new faces... and me.

After a brief statement regarding the purpose of our gathering (to simply listen, provide support, and share ideas on how we might become better stepfathers), we spent a good portion of the time listening to and sharing ideas with John, our soon-to-be stepfather from last time.

As their wedding date approaches John's two future stepsons are terrorizing the home and school, especially in John's presence in the home. Both kids were sent home yesterday from school for fighting with peers.

"I don't know what to do with them," muttered John. "I don't feel comfortable attempting to discipline them and not sure I would know how even if I did feel more at ease."

"What's going on with their old man?" asked Ron, a somewhat brash 26-year-old stepfather of two.

"I'm not sure, " replied John. "The kids occasionally talk to him by phone, but he is not really involved. Trina, my fiancee, despises the man and has made every effort to keep the boys away from him."

"Are you truly prepared for what you're about to do?" questioned Roy, another newcomer and seven-year veteran of the stepfamily wars. "Those two kids are resentful of you for not only causing their father to stay away, but they're probably afraid you'll take their mom away too."

"But I've treated those kids like gold!" cried John.

"Yea, but they can't see that right now. They will in time if you hang in there with them," replied Gene, another newcomer. "They're lashing out at the world right now, not you as a person. They are hurt and angry at their mom too. Those kids simply can't express it in any other way except to act out their anger."

"What do I do?" questioned John.

"Roll up your sleeves and dig in!" sounded Roy. "Let those kids know that no matter how tough it gets you ain't going anywhere. Then do it… every day, show them that you'll practice what you preach. If you do, they will come around, but it will take some time and a great deal of patience."

The brotherhood… the stepfathers "hood" was born tonight…

Thought for the Day: Grown men have been brought together since the beginning of time to fight battles, build nations, invent machines, build companies, and create games. Men have a long history of pulling together in victory. The commitment to excellence is ingrained in us. Our focus can be razor-sharp. All that's ever needed is a worthy cause… and a little popcorn and Pepsi.

American history is replete with examples of men of business who dreamed dreams and saw visions with the result that the economy of the nation was advanced. Faith is not listed in the index of many textbooks on economics, but one cannot read the lives of the great entrepreneurs without realizing that faith was one element they all had in common. They all have evidence of "things not seen."

I. E. Howard

The poor man is not he who is without a cent, but he who is without a dream.

Harry Kemp

Day # 253 Just When You Thought You Had It All Figured Out…

At every crossway on the road that leads to the future, each progressive spirit is opposed by a thousand men appointed to guard the past.

Anonymous

Our third meeting… week three of the "stepfathers' hood", our fast-becoming, sacred Thursday ritual… What happened? Where did we go wrong?

Only four players showed up tonight … not enough to have a good scrimmage! And yet, just because nine were present for our second meeting I assumed the numbers would triple every week, huh? Well, you go with what you got, and in the mean time double-check the TV log to make sure the NBA has not switched to Thursday nights.

I'm concerned because John was not here tonight. I hope last week's focus of attention on his family did not scare him off. Some of the guys were pretty up front and to the point with him.

Paul did return. He and I are the only three-time members of our newly formed brotherhood. I like Paul. We're as different as night and day, yet similar in so many ways when it comes to our views on stepparenting. Paul is having a difficult time with his biological kids, boys ages fourteen and eleven. As you recall, Paul has custody of his sons two weekends/month. He recently remarried and has a 12-year-old stepdaughter.

"I really don't get it," Paul states. "My two boys and I used to be so close, so intense with each other. We rode bikes together, played ball, went fishing… you name it. We were inseparable on weekends when they came to visit me. Now, it's as if they're going through the motions. They want nothing to do with me, opting instead to go somewhere with their friends. I just don't understand."

"How old did you say your boys were?" questioned Bill, a newcomer.

"Fourteen and eleven," replied Paul.

"My boys are a little bit older than yours," Bill continued, "but I remember going through the same thing with them after my divorce. They visited on weekends and wanted nothing to do with me either. I couldn't figure them out. They wouldn't tell me anything."

"So what did you do?" Paul asked curiously.

"Well, for one thing I quit trying to include them in all the weekend activities. I mean they were still expected to follow rules, be ready for church, eat Sunday dinner and so on. But I started making Saturdays special just for them. We would sit down on Friday evenings as soon as they arrived, and the three of us would decide what we were going to do on Saturday. Planning a special activity, even if it wasn't all that special… just the notion that they were in charge of Saturday gave them something to look forward to, and it insured quality time for the three of us even if the activity only lasted a couple of hours. I'll admit… it helps to have a wife who understands the situation and is willing to go along with the program. After all, she has worked all week too, and keeping up with her two kids is a full-time job!

"Pretty soon, my boys didn't see my new family as such a threat. It took time and patience, and talking to each other… to my wife and even constant explaining to my two stepsons. My wife and I made a commitment to keep the lines of communication open… to keep talking no matter what. As a result our Sunday afternoons are much smoother, actually downright fun at times. My boys, once they got over the fear that I was not going to lose sight of their lives, they have enjoyed being part-time big brothers to my two stepkids."

Who says quantity is important? Quality is always a winner. The four of us men learned a great deal about the significance of talking to our spouses and to our kids. We also learned that even though we may not be the biological parent, as males we're still viewed as head of the household. Our leadership is needed even when we proud members of the male species don't honestly know which direction to lead. As Paul and Bill pointed out tonight, where we lead is not always as significant as accepting the responsibility of leading and sometimes being man enough with our spouses and our kids to say, "Help, I'm lost; we're lost. Let's all sit down and figure out where it is we're going... where it is we want to go as a family."

It takes a big man to admit that he's lost. It takes an intelligent man to be at peace with himself while searching for direction. It takes a wise man to ask God for guidance and strength along the way.

Prayer: God, grant me the serenity to accept the things I cannot change, courage to change the things I can, and wisdom to know the difference.

And Heavenly Father, teach me to truly understand the significance of this simple, yet powerful prayer.

Day # 260 Do the Right Thing for the Right Reason...

Change means movement, movement means friction,
friction means heat, and heat means controversy. The
only place where there is no friction is in outer space or a
seminar on political action.
Saul Alinsky

I checked the TV log and Thursday nights still look good. I mean we're still competing with ESPN's "The NFL's Greatest Teams" weekly segment, college basketball, not to mention Clint Eastwood reruns on TNT; and if nothing else, just the sheer thrill of running up and down 47 channels at a clip of 17 channels/minute with TVbutt...

that's on a slow night. The average American male, once he's warmed up, or better yet, mad at his wife or kids... your average autistic Joe can easily hit a 27 channel/ minute clip and maintain such for at least 15 minutes... or until the little woman hurls a coffee cup at the TV screen! I spent three years working with autistic children, and I've yet to recall an autistic child's self-stimulatory behavior that could compete with man's repetitive rampage with TVbutt.

Anyway, we must have done something right last week. We're back to a nine-member crew this week, including John. Yes, he's still planning on stepfatherhood in the very near future. We haven't scared him off yet!

Tonight the focus of our attention was one of man's greatest enemies — work. It seems that man's nature is to engulf himself in his work, even if he seemingly doesn't care much for the actual work itself. It's a competitive thing. Adam should have never listened to Eve about that apple.

"My boss has absolutely no empathy for my new family situation," stated Andrew. "In fact I think he is jealous of my genuine interest in my wife's feelings. He can't fathom why I no longer want to spend extra time at the office or why happy hour to me no longer means spending time with the boys."

Andrew is a rookie stepfather... a rookie husband. In fact, Andrew is about as green as they come, even more so than John, and that makes John feel good! Yet, all of us old-timers admire Andrew's enthusiasm, his courage... his raw guts and honesty.

"I told my boss the other day that I had no desire to travel with the company. I apologized to him. Six months ago I was the chosen one for the promotion, and I was being groomed for the position on the road... the position that would require frequent overnight travel. I told him my priorities had changed the day I said, 'I do' three months ago. My family comes first before my job or my career for that matter. My boss thought that my honeymoon would end soon, and I would be back on his team; rah rah the company... you know how that goes don't you? But, I flat out told him no yesterday. I was not interested in the job even though the money and prestige would have been nice."

Andrew was a breath of fresh air tonight. Andrew gave some of us a wake-up call tonight. He reminded us that life is quite simple if you prioritize your values… God and family must come before the office. Once you get that established, you simply… as Andrew put it, "Do the right thing for the right reasons."

The rookie was definitely the MVP tonight.

Thought for the Day: *For where your treasure is, there your heart will be also.*

Matthew 6:21

Prayer: Father, thanks for rookies like Andrew. Please Father, don't let us old coots destroy his youthful exhuberance towards life, towards family… towards his commitment to values. Rather, grant us the courage to open our old eyes, to reach down into the very depths of our souls, knowing too, that we can be reborn by opening our hearts to You… the way, the truth, the light…

And Father, about our old, overweight bodies…

A Prayer For Old Age

Lord, thou knowest better than I know myself that I am old and growing older. Keep me from the fatal habit of thinking that I must say something on every subject and on every occasion. Release me from craving to straighten out everybody's affairs.

Make me thoughtful but not moody; helpful but not bossy. With my store of wisdom it seems a pity not to use it all, but Thou knowest that I want a few friends at the end. Keep me from the recital of endless details; give me wings to get to the point.

Seal my lips on my aches and pains. They are increasing, and love for rehearsing them is becoming sweeter as the years go by. I dare not ask for grace enough to enjoy the details of others' aches and pains, but help me to endure them with patience. I dare not ask for improved memory, but rather I ask for a growing humility and a lessening cocksureness when my memory seems to clash with the memory of others.

Teach me the gracious lesson that occasionally I may be mistaken. Keep me reasonably sweet. I do not want to be a saint; some of them are so hard to live with, but a sour old person is one of the crowning works of the devil.

Give me the ability to see good things in unexpected places and talents in unexpected people. Give me the grace to tell them so.

Author Unknown

Day # 265 The Over the Hill Gang…

Sonny Jerguson and company… a bunch of overweight, over-achieving coots who won the hearts of every middle-aged, arm-chair quarterback a generation ago. Pot-bellied Sonny and his band of renegades, led by their never-say-you're-too-old-to-play coach, George Allen, won game after game on faith, guts, and all-for-one/one-for-all glory. They knew how to win, and win they did whipping teams with players much younger and stronger.

I noticed my stepdaughters giggling when I meandered through the house today with my shirt off.

"What's so funny?" I asked.

"Oh, nothing dad. It's just…"

"Just what?" I hastily replied as I sucked in my slowly expanding middle-aged belly, sensing they were laughing at my over-the-hill body.

"They think you could use a bra!" laughed Donna, my wife.

"We didn't say that!" the girls gleefully replied. But the damage had been done. My ego had been bruised.

A lesser man would have buckled under such intense scrutiny. A

107

lesser man would have faked an injury to get taken out of this game, given the likes of his opposition.

I was considering just that, yet before I could start the bad back routine something inside of me stirred. The gimpy back gave way to a gleam in my eye. The girls and my wife could see it too.

"What?"

"Yea, what are you smiling about dad?"

"You still got that old skateboard?" I asked.

"Yea, in the garage, but…" stuttered my girls.

"You're not?" questioned Donna.

I shouldn't have…

Thought for the Day: Us members of the over-the-hill gang would be wise to remain so… and not make futile attempts to rejoin the likes of the young and "healable".

No question, we need regular exercise, a good diet, and lots of bran to even maintain our over-the-hill status, else we may baloon to big belly status. However, the over-the-hill senility prayer should be carried in one's tattered (and empty!) wallet at all times… for those occasions when we become delusional and think we're 25 years old again… Heck, even 35 sounds pretty good at times!

The Over-the-hill Gang Senility Prayer

God, grant me the brain cells to recollect that I'm not what I used to be.

The slight-of-mind to fake an old injury when tempted by youth.

The sensation to know when I'm faking and when I'm really hurting.

The warmth of spirit to enjoy the memories of my playing days.

The courage to always remain young at heart… And,

The wisdom to truly "see" with my heart what is important in this game we call life.

Thought for the Home Stretch:

And God Said "No"

I asked God to take away my pride, and God said, "No". He said it was not for Him to take away, but for me to give up.

I asked God to make my handicapped child whole, and God said, "No". He said her spirit is whole, her body only temporary.

I asked God to grant me patience, and God said, "No". He said that patience is a by-product of tribulation; it isn't granted, it's earned.

I asked God to give me happiness, and God said, "No". He said He gives blessings. Happiness is up to me.

I asked God to spare my pain, and God said, "No". He said suffering draws you apart from worldly cares and brings you closer to Me.

I asked God to make my spirit grow, and God said, "No". He said I must grow on my own, but He will prune me to make me fruitful.

I asked God if He loved me, and God said, "Yes". He gave His only begotten Son who died for me, and I will be in heaven some day because I believe.

I ask God to help me love others as much as He loves me, and God said, "Ah, finally you have the right idea."

Anonymous

"When my 12-year-old refuses to go to bed, what do I do?"

9

the home stretch

broth-er-hood: 1. "hood" thing. **2.** association; fraternity. **3.** a biological necessity for the male species, and can occur outside the realm of a playing field if popcorn and Pepsi are available and an occasional belch is acceptable. Tears? Maybe, but no hugs please... too much touchy feely stuff tarnishes the macho image.

ma-nip-u-la-tion: 1. to influence, especially with intent to deceive. **2.** a behavior management concept where the parents use rewards to instill desired behavior in their children. **3.** when teenagers turn the tide and use the art of filibuster to get what they want from their parents.

Day # 274 The Bomb…

It was a beautiful fall day… not a cloud in the sky. I was excited, yet nervous as I ran from my fifth grade class to the huge playground at First Lutheran School. The big boys, the seventh and eighth graders, had already started the football game, but I was allowed in the game, unknown to the other team that I could fly! Jimmy knew… our eighth grade quarterback. My first play in the huddle, I could see that gleam in Jimmy's eyes. It meant only one thing — The Bomb!

I strutted out to the flanker position, doing my best Charley Taylor/Raymond Berry imitations. The ball was snapped. I bolted towards the endzone… what seemed like an eternity… in reality only a 30-yard dash. Jimmy let that football fly as far as he could fling it. I saw it falling from the sky, churning as fast as I could go until finally I caught up with it… and the endzone hedge/fence at the same time! The emaculate reception in the annals of First Lutheran football history… The kid had arrived.

Some thirty years and 30,000 yards later, I'm throwing bombs to my stepdaughters in the backyard. Lance Alworth they ain't; Joe Kapp I am… not a true spiral to be found in my old right arm. Yet, the thrill is still there when an over-the-shoulder catch is made.

Some thirty years and one week later, my lovely stepdaughters are throwing bombs to me, however, these bombs are not of the gridiron variety. These bombs are of the emotional variety… bombs that have strong feelings, like backtalking me, openly defying my authority as the quarterback… the coach. Bombs like refusing to run the right routes, opting to break off from the play that was called to do their own thing. Imagine that…

Everyone knows teenagers are going to test the waters and defy authority. That's part of their rite of passage as they approach young adulthood. But, that doesn't make me, the coach, any happier or easier to deal with, especially when the defiance reaches bomblike proportions. Why should I have to deal with it? Why not just bench them, or better yet, kick them off the team! I signed a lifelong contract with their mom, but does that mean I have to keep getting blitzed and bombed by them? I haven't done that much to deserve such treatment. What do they expect from me?

Boom! Another bomb dropped… They told their friend on the phone, within my earshot of course, that I was mean to them and did not care about them, only their mom. They were just part of the package deal, and I was tired of the excess baggage. Should I call a huddle or time-out? Or should I concede defeat? Change the playbook and prepare for next week's battles and bombs? Perhaps it's time I chatted with my Coach, my Creator. He might even consult with The Bear or Knute on this one…

> ***Thought for the Day:*** *The Good Lord can make you anything you want to be, but you have to put everything in His hands.*
> *Mahalia Jackson*

Day # 277 Game Film

I had a talk with my Coach. He listened with compassion, with concern… with unconditional love. And, as usual, He did not offer any new plays to my playbook. He rarely does. He tends to talk to me more in terms of philosophy, and lets me draw up the plays. It's kind of funny when I think about it… If He called a specific play, I'd probably call an audible… just like my stepdaughters, huh! The old man is as defiant as his stepkids. Coach knows this and turns the tide (sorry, Bear) by getting me to "see" the philosophy and what it takes to win, yet He still puts the responsibility for my actions back on me. It's my call, my play.

But wait a minute. He's taking this session to a deeper level. He's telling me to close the playbook and my eyes.

Be still…

I'm seeing game film of my life. A highlight film it ain't… more like a horror movie, at least the clips He's showing me. Some of the worst play-calling you can imagine, and yet, every time I crawl off the field of play He's there. Always there… with compassion, with concern, with love. He has benched me more than a few times but never kicked me off His team. In fact, He continually tells me I have a permanent place on His team. So what's He trying to tell me?

Be still…

The game film suddenly changes. I'm seeing clips of Jesus as He roamed the earth. Poetry in motion, never once throwing an interception… nary a fumble; only one unsportsmanlike call in thirty-three years, and most agree He was justified in turning over the tables at the temple. Meanwhile, His players fumbled, dropped passes, jumped offsides, ran the wrong routes… you name it they committed every penalty and turnover in the playbook. But Jesus never flinched.

Be still…

The game film changes again… I see a gray-haired man with a gleam in his eye as he watches his youngest son run the bases, throw the football, shoot the basketball. Only three times in my thirty-one years on this earth in his presence was he guilty of unsportsmanlike conduct toward me. And he always aproached me afterwards and apologized with a tear in his eye. How many times I must have hurt his feelings, committed a foul… you name it, yet he was always there. Always to the end. He sacrificed so much of his life for me.

Be still…

The scene changes one more time… to my home, my den and my once new couch/loveseat before my two stepmuts took them over. I can see them draped across the couch as I walk in. Only an hour earlier, I had taken my frustrations out on both of them… as if they had anything to do with the mess I had been trying to clean up at work. I had fussed. I had fumed. I had put them down in the basement. Now, as I'm walking in to relax, I see them looking at me, not with fear or anger in their eyes… just a smile on each of their hairy faces. Dog smiles and a pair of tails wagging. I was the jerk an hour earlier, and here they were approaching me as if I had just hung the moon… the same way they approached me every morning and every night — as if the past never existed.

The film session has ended. I'm left sitting in the darkness to ponder the meaning of it all when I get that feeling… that fibration in my gut that tells me Coach is about to drop the bomb on me. Again, not necessarily the answer or the specific play; just the philosophy, the concept… the correct game plan.

Be still…

In the darkness I feel the warmth, the glow, the answer to my stepdaughters' bombs. Detonate them with love of the unconditional kind. No contingencies, no screen passes, no "win one for the Gipper" speeches. Just let my girls know that regardless of the magnitude of their bombs, I will always be there waiting for them… just like my Coach, just like my dad, just like my dogs. That's not to say consequences won't occur. That's not to say disciplinary action will be soft. But, my reaction must come from my connection to unconditional love, not from my anger or resentment.

How does one achieve such understanding and patience… and love? Is it ever feasible to think the non-biological parent can exemplify unconditional love and acceptance? After all, these two stepdaughters of mine are not my flesh and blood. And besides, the whole world is conditional… Do unto others as they have done unto you. That's the modern-day version of the Golden Rule, right?

It's time to start the film again. Turn out the lights.

Be still…

Thought for the Day: "Love is patient, love is kind. It does not envy, it does not boast, it is not proud. It is not rude, it is not self-seeking, it is not easily angered, it keeps no record of wrongs. Love… rejoices with the truth. It always protects, trusts, hopes, perseveres. Love never fails…   *I Corinthians 13:4-8 (NIV)*

Day # 281 Halftime Adjustments

My heart was troubled as I arrived at the clubhouse tonight. I needed to hear from the other stepfathers in the group. How did they deal with this notion of unconditional love? Did they also feel guilty at times, as I do, because of the ever-increasing feelings of anger and resentment? Anger and resentment due not only to kid defiance but also due to the lack of respect they show me. In their eyes my schedule, my goals and dreams, my privacy, my Pepsi in the frig… they just don't seem to matter. So why should I break my neck to meet their seemingly endless list of demands and expectations?

"Joe, when was the last time you and your wife got away from it all for a day or two?" asked Roy. "You look like you could use some time away, especially from your girls."

"Sounds good, but it's not possible in the near future. Besides, the last time we got away for a weekend our kids managed to screw up the first night by not being where they were suppose to be. For the rest of the weekend, my wife could not enjoy the trip for fear her girls were getting into some kind of trouble… as if every teenager doesn't 'sow some oats' when their parents go out of town. That's normal isn't it? I agree… there's a limit to what should be allowed, but I don't see it the same way Donna sees it. I get angry at the kids because I see what it's doing to Donna. Anyway, getting away at this point and time is out of the question."

"Why are you so angry?" fired Bob.

"I'm not sure… I'm not even sure who I'm angry at the most… me or the kids. When I take a step back from the battle or discussion or whatever 'exchange' has occurred, I realize they're just kids… teenagers wanting to have it their way. I'm not used to players being so defiant, yet, that's not really the heart of the matter. What bothers me is the way I respond to them. It's so conditional at times… I'll be friendly to you if you clean your room, if you quit taping over my 20-year-old music tapes, if you tell your friends to quit calling after midnight… on and on, and with every rule violation or even simple mistake I emotionally detach myself from them. Heck, I shut down and flat out ignore their existence. They know I'm mad. I know they know. Yet, I can't bring myself to resolve it until a few days later when I feel like a dog for acting that way, and then I approach them. My dad never waited that long to 'make up' with me. Twenty minutes was his limit, and he was in my room with a tear in his eye talking to me. Why can't I do that with my girls? Why is my love for them seemingly so conditional? I know I care about them, and I know if their mother died tomorrow, I wouldn't walk out on them. I'd be there for them. But I honestly don't know if I would be doing it out of love or out of a sense of it's the right thing to do."

"You will never feel the unconditional love like your wife feels for her kids," commented Robert. "I've got two biological children and two stepchildren, all within the same age range. I'm like you. I know that I would take care of my stepkids no matter what, but there's no way I will ever feel the same bond… the same kinship that I feel with my biological kids. I'm not sure any stepparent can feel that bond or even understand the level of unconditional love that I'm referring to."

"I agree," said Thomas. "After five years of stepfamilyhood, we've come to the realization that our bonds are different and that's okay. In fact, we use it to our advantage. The stepparent, being more detached, can often see situations from a more objective point of view and can subsequently help the 'real' parent take a step back emotionally. When it comes to allowing kids to make decisions and experience consequences, the stepparent can be a big help… a buffer for the biological parent who often wants to control the child too much."

"Yea, the love will blossom over time," added James. "It took several years of strugglng with the notion of unconditional love before I came to terms with my stepchildren, especially my stepdaughter. We men sometimes forget that our daughters are suffering great loss at the time of divorce. Boys suffer the loss too, but there's something to be said for the loss the girls feel when dad is no longer around and mom is living with and sleeping with another man. Not only is the daughter grieving over the loss of her real father, not to mention the fact that she's probably blaming herself for the divorce. She is also grieving the loss of her mom. After all, this new ceature called stepdad is monopolyzing mom's time and attention… She no longer feels cared for or needed."

"I know the feeling all too well," said Brent. "I've got a biological daughter who I see regularly and I have a stepdaughter who spends weekends and summers with her father. I feel for both of them… their pain is still present even though we've had this arrangement now for four years. I love 'em both dearly, but I'm not going to lie to you… the love I feel for my biological daughter runs much deeper. Yet, my love for my stepdaughter has grown over time, no question about that. We've been together since she was seven years old. That makes a difference too, you know. I didn't start with teenagers like you did, Joe. That makes it doubly tough. They're already at that stage of rebellion, not to mention all the 'step baggage' that continually grows."

Unconditional love… I'm still not sure I know what it is, but at least I know I'm not alone in my search for the truth. I've got my teammates here at the clubhouse. I've got my Coach and the Playbook. I've got the game film as a reminder.

I think I'm finally on the right path…

Thought for the Day: Character cannot be developed in ease and quiet. Only through experience of trial and suffering can the soul be strengthened.

Helen Keller

*Far away there in the sunshine are my highest
aspirations. I may not reach them, but I can look up
and see their beauty. believe in them, and try
to follow where they lead.*
Louisa May Alcott

Combine a tough mind with a tender heart.
Martin Luther King

Day # 286 Single Parenting…

We're several weeks away from our first real family vacation. We're going to the beach… back to Ocean Boulevard West where my love affair with the ocean was born. I can't wait.

The girls seem excited too, genuinely so. According to Donna, they've never really experienced a family vacation. Donna spent much of their childhood years raising them by herself. From her perspective, there's something missing in the notion of a vacation when your kids are young and you take them on a trip by yourself. I can appreciate that point of view much better now.

I'm sometimes amazed that I'm a stepfather. Yet, true amazement sets in when I try to imagine myself raising two kids alone. Some men do it… probably more than I'm aware of. Many women do it. Regardless of which parent does it, what an incredible feat to think that a human being in this day and time can earn a living and raise a family alone.

It's sad that so many kids and single parents live that way. It was not meant to be done alone. I wonder how many single parents jump into relationships too fast as a result of the overwhelming loneliness and responsibility they shoulder? I wonder how many single parents vow never to marry again because the last go-around was so traumatic? I wonder how many kids of divorce will wind up divorced some day? We always think that we'll never do to our own that which was so painful to us as kids, and yet...

Prayer: Dear Heavenly Father, please bless the single parents in this land. Assign them a guardian angel to watch over them... to watch over their kids. Regardless of who's to blame that so many of these parents are alone, they need Your love and understanding, Your guiding light, Your Son, Jesus, to enter their lives.

Give them hope Father. Give them strength. And, if at all possible, give them a soulmate to spend eternity with... someone like You sent me. They deserve it.

Day # 301 The Road to the FeatherZone...

We're settling into a solid routine in our Stepfathers' Anonymous meetings. It still amazes me grown men from various walks of life can honestly check their egos at the door for the greater cause of the group — becoming better stepfathers.

Tonight we wandered through the various stages that stepfathers unknowingly travel through on the road to the FeatherZone. We talked at length about the significance of establishing trust with our kids, and there seemed to be several key means of gaining trust. First, we had to establish a simple friendship with our stepchildren. All agreed making friends was not a 50-50 scenario... that we had to be willing to reach out to them no matter how much we were initially rejected by them.

"I don't know about you, but I've had a tougher time gaining the acceptance of my 14-year-old stepson. My 9-year-old stepdaughter bonded well with me. Establishing a friendship with her was a piece of cake compared to my boy," stated Marc, a two year veteran of the stepfamily scene.

"Yea, teenagers are definitely more close minded," chuckled James. "My two teenage stepdaughters took me for a ride for the first six months. I thought we were establishing a basis for friendship when in reality they were using me... manipulating me to get whatever they wanted. It's hard to establish a friendship when you're immediately thrust into disciplining kids, who by their very nature of adolescence, are going to be rebellious and manipulative."

Enough said! We all agreed that it was our responsibility to not give up on the possibility of establishing a simple friendship with our stepchildren. We had to be willing to go the exta mile and to keep a positive attitude in the face of rejection and rebellion along the way. Once a simple friendship was established, we could then start to tackle the issue of trust.

"Trust is simple," said Paul. "You simply have to do what you say you're going to do **every** time you say it in the initial phase. You've got to deliver the goods! If you can't deliver them, then by all means don't say you can, especially when teenagers are involved."

"But how long does it take to establish trust?" questioned Pete. "I've been good to my stepkids. I've been honest with them. Yet, they still don't trust me."

"It might take a lifetime... who knows," stated Charley.

Sometimes these meetings are painful. We realize our road to the FeatherZone is filled with various challenges and pitfalls. It's hard to imagine spending several years trying to get your stepkids to trust you. Yet, we have to remind ourselves we may never know or fully understand the relationship our stepchildren had or continue to have with their biological fathers. It may have been a wonderful, loving relationship that was abruptly taken away from the kids' point of view. Or perhaps that loving relationship continues on a part-time basis and we stepfathers will always be viewed as an unwelcomed outsider or intruder.

The other side of the coin may have also occurred. Our stepchildren may have been emotionally, physically or even sexually abused by their biological father. If he traumatized them in any way, and it happens far more frequently to both boys and girls than we want to acknowledge, how in the world can we stepfathers expect to gain trust?

We may never uncover the truth. It's not our job... not necessarily our purpose. Our job as stepfathers is to provide an example of Jesus' love to our stepkids. Better yet, introduce them to Christ's teachings and then consistently exemplify His love and teachings in our everyday encounters with them.

What better gift could we provide our stepchildren over the course of their lives?

Thought for the Day: Limits exist only in the mind, for with God **all** things are possible. Grasp that concept — take it to heart. There is no task or challenge beyond your reach. If you can visualize a solution, you can create an answer. That's God's gift to **all** who believe on His name and study His word... His Playbook.

For God hath not given us the spirit of fear, but of
power, and of love, and of sound mind.
II Timothy 1:7

Day # 308 Coach Who?

Our discussion last week regarding the stages of successful stepparenting picked up where it left off.

Once trust was established, it seemed only natural that we evolve into coaching or mentoring our stepchildren.

"We're not referring to coaching little league are we?" questioned John, who probably never held a baseball bat in his hands. After all... oops! Some of us forgot to check our egos at the door tonight. Just the word coach conjures up visions of locker room jargon and win one for the Bear speeches. Please excuse our momenary lapse into beasthood...

"Mentoring seems to have more to do with establishing credibility and trust with our stepkids that they are willing to solicit our advice," stated Paul, who was fast becoming our resident philosopher (there goes that jealous ego again!).

Our group had no problem grasping the notion of mentoring as a step along the path to the FeatherZone. What kept getting in the way was discipline... When was it okay to discipline my stepkids was the most frequently asked question tonight. It must have been a rough week for all.

Us old timers in the group knew the answer, but we were wise enough to let the discussion go... to let the group struggle with this dilemma. After all, it's perhaps the toughest issue we face in dealing with our stepchildren, not to mention the fact that everyone's circumstances are unique. The major concensus among the group was not so much when we as stepfathers started to discipline our stepchildren... it was how we did it and to what extent we formed a partnership with our spouses in the process.

All agreed that to reach the FeatherZone we had to learn how to successfully discipline our stepchildren, stepteenagers included. It was essential that our kids experience some measure of "tough love" from us; that we cared enough about them to make them do the right thing as best we knew how. Tough love was viewed as hanging tough with our kids, not giving in to their manipulations or succumbing to their barrage of demands due to fatigue or a lack of genuine concern.

If we wanted to develop a sincere, caring relationship with our stepchildren, they had to know we could not only be trusted. They also had to know we would not wilt under their pressure... that we had the courage to go the distance with them.

Sounds good... go team!

"But I still don't understand. When my 12-year-old stepson refuses to go to bed what do I do?" a truly puzzled Roy asked.

Meeting adjourned! Whew! Us wise old men of the group had no idea what to tell Roy. We better do some homework before next week's meeting. Roy's coming back...

Thought for the Day: Just what do you do when your 12-year-old stepson challenges you to a duel?

> *I believe that the first test of a truly great man is his humility. I do not mean, by humility, doubt of his power. But really great men have curious feeling that the greatness is not in them, but through them. And they see something divine in every other man and are endless, foolishly incredibly merciful.*
> *John Ruskin*

Day # 312 Helpless...

While trying to figure out what to tell Roy next week about his 12-year-old stepson's refusal to go to bed, I kinda got sidetracked, or maybe I should say sideswiped! My 17-year-old stepdaughter is not refusing to go to bed. Nothing that serious... She's simply refusing to come home tonight! She has decided to spend the night with a group of friends, all girls of course. If your 17-year-old told you after missing curfew that she was not coming home tonight... that she was spending the night with a bunch of girls even though she left the house earlier with her boyfriend, you'd believe her wouldn't you? After all, I've spent all this time establishing trust. I can't imagine my stepdaughter lying to me can you?

Meanwhile, I've got to contain Donna before she calls 911, the National Guard, or worse yet... her father who owns a shotgun.

Maybe I can comfort Roy this week by telling him that 12-year-olds can be picked up and put into bed. Seventeen-year-old stepdaughters cannot. Seventeen-year-old stepdaughters cannot even be made to come home. And when she does come home, what am I going to do… ground her for two weeks and then sit and guard her room so she doesn't climb out the window?

Her mom's idea is to ground her until she turns eighteen (about nine months from now!) and tell the boyfriend to take a hike. Yea, that will work, I'm sure…

Thought for the Day: What goes around, comes around… again! Why does this thought keep resurfacing?

Prayer: Father, I'm trying to look beneath the surface… to not simply judge the outward behavior this time, but it just ain't working. The more I look beneath the surface, the more I want to panic… to throw up my hands in disgust. And all this is taking place while my 14-year-old stepdaughter watches to see how we handle the situation. You mean to tell me she's going to do the same thing when she gets older?

Father, I know not what to do except ask Your guardian angels to watch over Shannon tonight. Keep her safe. And send another angel over to knock Donna out so we can get some peace around here.

Your family is grown up when your kids stop asking you where they came from and refuse to tell you where they're going.
Jacob M. Braude

Day # 315 Who's Managing Who?

Roy returned tonight to our meeting but the puzzled look had changed to a look of supreme confidence.

"What happened with your 12-year-old?" we asked curiously.

"Well, he's going to bed, no problem," replied Roy. "Jim and I got together after last week's meeting and tossed around some ideas.

"Yea, I was having a similar problem with my 9-year-old stepson," stated Jim, a quiet, unassuming member of our group. "I set up a contract with my boy. If he went to bed on time each night, he earned five points. For every time that I had to remind him to either get in bed or go back to bed, I deducted a point. If he lost all five points on any given night, he automatically received early bedtime the following night. At the end of each week, he could cash in his points for prizes. If he scored a perfect 35 points, he had a grand prize list to choose from. Now, I don't have to fight with him. I just remind him that it's his choice what he earns... and most importantly, he knows I'll stick to my guns and not give in at the end of the week. Things really fell into place after I enforced the early bedtime rule a few times and did not give him unearned points at the end of the week."

"I tried it last week with my 12-year-old," stated Roy, "and I was amazed at how well he responded. Jim and I agree that we'll have to keep spicing up the payoff list every month or so, but that's a lot easier than going into battle."

Gee, I wonder if this idea would work with my 17-year-old? For every time she comes home on time, I'll... I'd hate to see her payoff list. Besides, she would figure out some loophole in the system...

Thought for the Day: When utilizing behavior management techniques on your children, do you ever wonder who's manipulating who?

Day # 319 Let go... Let God

Shannon came back as if nothing ever happened the other night. Her mom told her she was grounded for two weeks, but it went in one ear and out the other. She knows we're not going to stand guard every night for two weeks. She's right. We'd go crazy if we tried...

We'll do as we usually do — demand that she toll the line for a few days, take the phone away... which she gets anyway and then blames her sister for sneaking the phone in her room. Shannon will play along, all the while knowing that in 72 hours she'll be free to go back to what she was doing.

Twelve years of managing the toughest teenagers in the state and I can't seem to manage my own stepdaughter. Why is that? Perhaps if I received a salary for my overtime work as a stepdad… No, I'd have to fire myself for inconsistency and failure to stand up to the barrage of manipulations (pitches) she throws at us. She is still the best pitcher I ever faced! Let's face it… my 17-year-old has my number and I might as well accept the fact that I cannot control her.

I can still care for her. I can still try to exemplify Jesus' teachings and love for her. And I can make sure my 14-year-old doesn't fully comprehend my throwing in the towel on her older sister. I've still got her fooled for the moment… or do I?

Let's face it (again)… my 14-year-old has me right where she wants me. Jamie has me wrapped around her little finger. Where her older sister is bold, in-your-face defiant at times, Jamie is smooth. She kills me with kindness and writes me notes… and calls me dad.

The cold, hard reality is this… after almost ten months of stepparenting, I'm whooped! I concede. I'm no match for these two.

Prayer: Father, forgive me for conceding defeat to my two step-daughters. I'm not giving up on them. I'm simply recognizing my limitations as a stepfather. These two are much wiser than their respective years on this earth… much wiser and more sophisticated than those tough kids I worked with years ago. Help me to let go of my concern about control; to accept the fact they have minds of their own and regardless of what I think, they've got to find out some things for themselves. Just keep Your guardian angels with them Father. They're still kids trying to learn the ropes of a very cruel adult world. Guide them. Keep them safe. And let them know I'll always be there for them… I'll never turn my back on them. I may turn a deaf ear to their verbal barrage, but I'll always care. I'll always love them. After ten months, I do know that much.

And Father, thank you so much for providing me the opportunity to be a stepfather... to experience both the joys and the pains, the laughter and the lonliness... the love. I feel so blessed to have the chance to be a stepparent, knowing that I can always be there for them as they grow into adulthood and leave the nest to make it on their own. They will leave some day won't they?

Finally Father, I'm forever grateful to You for putting Donna in my path. I've got a partner for life... and eternity. Just please don't put us in charge of daycare when we get to heaven. Donna will have them grounded for years while I'm letting them off the hook!

When God made mother, He must have laughed with satisfaction, and framed it quickly — so rich, so deep, so divine, so full of soul, power, and beauty was the conception.
Henry Ward Beecher

Husbands are awkward things to deal with; even keeping them in hot water will not make them tender.
Mary Buckley

Day # 329 The Old High School Cheer...

What a meeting tonight. Do you remember back to high school, sitting out in the cold during a football game or in the old gymnasium during a basketball game, and the cheerleaders leading the old school colors cheer?

"Give me a blue! Give me a white! Blue! White! Everybody chose a color and screamed, right? I mean no one actually called both colors.

We had that kind of meeting tonight. On one side we had the

129

blues… the stepfathers crying the blues about sibling and stepsibling rivalry.

"I'm up to here with the way my stepsons treat my daughter when she comes to visit," complained Bob. "She is part of this family… my family, my flesh and blood, and I expect her to be treated as such."

On the other side we had the whites… the stepfathers crying foul about the way the biological parents handle visitation.

"He ain't nothin' but white trash. He don't deserve to see my two stepsons every month. He treats them like dirt and tries to convince them I'm no good," cries Doug. "If I thought I could get by with it I'd go over there and punch his lights out!"

Yea! The blues return the cheer.

"My 16-year-old stepdaughter refuses to baby-sit our new son," stammers William. "Can you imagine that? Why, I've worked over-time to buy her makeup and clothes, yet she's so selfish she won't watch our baby one night so that her mother and I can enjoy an evening out. Just one night out! Betty and I thought she would enjoy having a younger half-sister around. But, ever since the baby arrived eight months ago, she acts like the baby has the plague. Sure, the baby gets most of our attention, but my stepdaughter was always on the phone or with one of her girlfriends anyway. I just don't get it."

The whites come back even louder. Jim, the quiet one with the flair for behavior contracting, speaks out… "My wife hates my ex-wife. She cannot stand the thought of my girls spending a weekend with their mother. We took custody last year because she was never around to take care of the girls. Now, she's fought to get monthly weekend visits… probably out of spite. I don't see her making any kind of genuine effort to spend quality time with the girls. In the meantime she calls our house to talk to the girls and gives my wife a tough time. Whew! If those two ever got in the same room, it would look like an Ali-Frazier fight!"

All night it was the blues, then the whites, and each scenario got louder, just like the old cheer. Nonstop for almost two hours… like a bunch of old hens. Who would have thought a group of dignified stepfathers quietly meeting to discuss alternative ways to become better stepparents could lower themselves to this level of communication. Needless to say, we had a ball!

Thought for the Day: If there is any great secret of success in life, it lies in the ability to put yourself in the other person's place and to see things from his point of view — as well as your own.
Henry Ford

When stepparenting we sometimes forget to look at what's going on from our kids' perspective. Granted, we've got family feuds to referee, family budgets to balance, bosses wanting more of our time at the office, wives wanting more intimate conversation, not to mention the cars to keep running, the shower doors to fix... We've got a full plate, and on top of it all we're constantly battling our biological battles and desires to binge and lounge in the recliner with TVbutt, oblivious to the world of family around us.

But what about our kids? What does their plate look like. Besides their inborn desires to keep a phone to their ears while blaring Beevis and Butthead on the tube, they're often dealing with a garden variety serving... possibly as many as four parents, five or six siblings or part-time stepsiblings, two homes, four pets, not to mention the unusual and customary childhood/adolescent issues, which, all too often, include tremendous feelings of guilt over the break-up of their nuclear families. And we haven't even mentioned the one in four kids who has experienced the nightmares of abuse, neglect, or a family ripped open by alcoholism or drug addiction...

Get the picture dad? As stepfathers we must learn to juggle our day-to-day variables in such a way that we save as much emotional support and love for our kids as possible. What's left over, and let's face it... in most relationships it needs to be a healthy serving of leftovers... what's left goes to our partner, our spouse, and the leftovers need to be warm, not cold.

Where's the gas station? Where do we fill up our tanks to start another day or to finish the day strong? There's only one true source of energy, and it ain't at the neighborhood watering hole. It's at the eternal filling station in the heavens. God is our service station and Jesus is the attendant. He will pump the gas, check under the hood, and even wash the windshield for good measure. All we've got to do is ask. And we can pay by credit card with no interest! Just simply open the Playbook... the Bible. and study it daily. Talk to our Creator and His Son daily. He's already signed the ticket. The bill was paid some 2000 years ago with His blood.

Some of us (men only, of course... the female species is on the verge of making the same mistake but still have time to turn the tide)... we macho, males with the huge egos attached to our personage often times have a difficult time "letting go and letting God" work in our lives. That's never to say that we simply stop striving to be the best that we can be. That's never to downplay the significance of courage and tenacity... hustle and assertiveness... and just downright nose to the grindstone toughness. What we fail to see is that it takes all of these qualities working together to reach the level of letting go that we need to succeed. Letting go does not mean giving up. On the contrary, "letting go and letting God" is working diligently towards the fulfillment of our goals and dreams, knowing and seeing that God is ultimately in charge... That He has our best interest at heart... that with Him, **all** things are possible, including the daily challenge of managing our families and meeting their needs to the fullest extent **every** day... day after day... week afer week... season afer season... the Cal Ripkens of the stepparenting world. Consistency with class and honor... and humility, always recognizing the true energy source.

I can do all things through Him who strengthens me.
Philippians 4:13

Home Sweet Home...

Oh give me a home
Where the children don't roam,
Where no kids and no radios sing.
Where never is heard
A loud M-TV blurb,
And the phones do not clatter or ring.

Home home on the range
Where the girls and the homeless dogs play.
Where rarely is heard
An enlightening word,
And the bills are so backed up, can't pay.

"God grant me the serenity to..."

10

on the path...

Step-fa-ther: 1. strong spiritually, yet sensitive emotionally; willing to coach and/or play back-up quarterback/relief pitcher. **2.** able to play within the rules as defined by the referee (biological mother). **3.** willing to sacrifice his entire being for the good of the team — the family; committed to the principle that no matter how big or small each member of his team should experience some measure of joy in their home lives every day. **4.** a strong sense of humor, with the ability to laugh at himself and laugh with his teammates. **5.** ultimately committed to exemplifying the love of Christ to his family. **6.** a man among men... a genuine role model.

Day # 334 Back in Paradise...

Grief can take care of itself, but to get the full value of joy you must have somebody to divide it with.

Mark Twain

Thought for the Day: When it's your first family vacation to the beach, and within the first two hours of an eleven-hour car ride you get a speeding ticket and your 17-year-old stepdaughter sends particles of her previously digested lunch all over the back of your head, should you continue or turn around and head home?

I remember my first trip to the beach as a 10-year-old kid with my family. I was in total disbelief when I saw the ocean for the very first time. I asked my older brother what had happened to the sides of the ocean... I guess I was expecting a huge pool.

Twenty-eight years later I am experiencing my first trip to the beach with **my** family. Like a child of ten, I'm wondering where the seagulls sleep at night. I'm fascinated watching the pelicans fly in formation just barely above the waves breaking. I see the gleam in my stepdaughters' eyes as they frolic in the ocean, seemingly carefree from the cruelties that the world has bestowed upon them.

Time seems to stand still at the ocean. There's only daylight and starlight... or perhaps moonlight. There's nothing like a late night walk on the beach with a full moon glistening above the sea. There's the pounding of the waves at high tide; serene calm at low tide. It's all coming back to me now. Beach time... It's worlds apart from the craziness of the city. It's no wonder I fell in love with this place last year when I was living here.

Yet, as beautiful as the memories are of sunsets on the beach, storms out over the ocean, waves forever crashing, I'm overwhelmed with the vast emptiness I felt living here in paradise by myself. I had no family. I had few friends. I was alone... just one short year ago.

Now look at me. I've got teenagers calling me dad. I've got a wife calling me various names. I've got dogs barking my name. I've got the weirdest group of teenage boys I've ever seen calling me "Mr." when they knock on my door. A few actually say, "Sir". Am I blest or what?

Prayer: Heavenly Father, the Creator, thank you so very much for creating our oceans and beaches. Help us to find ways to preserve their beauty and integrity.

Thanks for creating our senses, which allow us to feel the ocean breeze on a warm summer night; see the full moon cast its light over each breaking wave; smell the air; hear the waves forever roaring...

Thanks for creating the dolphin who gracefully swim off shore every morning; for the pelicans who remind us of the beauty of formation and order; for the tiny beach crabs who tell us all have a place in Your universe.

Father, thanks for this family, my family that You have linked me with. Just as You created the moon to control the tides, guide me as I attempt to lead this household. There will be storms. Teach me to steer through such times, always showing my new family sunny skies and gentle breezes are on the horizon.

Fill me with grace and humility, love and compassion, never to lose my playful side... Spirit-filled and childlike, father and husband, forever Your son.

Day # 344 Gutcheck Time...

It was a "take no prisoners" crowd tonight. The clubhouse was seething with anger. The subject was women... our wives. This was a R-rated meeting. Stepkids were not even in the line-up. Nope... every ounce of harbored hostility was the wives' doings, not ours. Sure, it takes two to rumble, but someone has got to strike the first blow and we didn't even call the principals together. We were content with our TV butts watching three games simultaneously... just minding our own business, self-stimming away.

"She didn't even ring the bell to start the fight!" cried Paul. "She just jumped in the ring and started pounding me... 'Why didn't you do this and why didn't you do that? And just what were you doing at lunch yesterday. I called and you were out!' I mean it went on and on nonstop for a good three rounds. She was throwing left hooks, upper cuts, even a few low blows among the bunch."

"So what did you do?" we stepfathers questioned in unity.

"Nothing. I told her to move away from the TV while she yelled... I was missing the games. And I kept clicking the buttons!"

"Yea! That showed her who was boss!" we yelled. "We'll talk when we're ready to talk!"

"I just don't understand her," sighed Frank. "She doesn't know how to fight fair with me. I say what's on my mind, get it out, make a decision about the situation, and then move on. Just do it! Why she feels a need to bring up three-week-old garbage I'll never know. Yesterday is gone."

"Yea, I really don't need this talking, touchy feely stuff after working a 10-hour day. I just need time to vegetate at home. I mean, she worked, sure, but it's not the same, you know. Just let me be me for awhile. I'll come around later in the evening... except on Monday nights when I'm watching football and Tuesday nights when the NBA is on TBS... Let's see, Wednesday around 8 P.M. looks pretty good, unless they're running a Clint Eastwood rerun."

"Get this, guys!" shouts Mark. "My wife wants me to go to a weekend couples retreat to learn how to express ourselves more openly. Can you imagine that? I might consider doing it in late July before football season kicks in, but she's wanting to go in two weeks... in the middle of the NBA Championship Series. What's with her? She knows every year I wait on that 7-game series, glued to the set for every game. I compromised with her this year and cut down on the number of regular season games, but the playoffs... the World Championship… the brass ring? Women just don't understand the significance of such events."

Male bonding gone awry? The building is about to erupt when… "Excuse me Mark, your wife's on the line."

In our feeding frenzied excitement, we did not hear the clubhouse phone ring. Poor Mark… What's he going to do? Will he save face among his peers and take a message, or will he henpeck himself into the history books?

"Excuse me fellas… I've got a call."

Silence has fallen on the throng.

A wake-up call has gone out.

Wild-eyed glee has changed to little boy bewilderment.

Not a word uttered in the clubhouse as Mark walks back in the room.

"Well?"

"Well, what?" clammered Mark.

"Well, what did she want?"

"She called to tell me she was taking the kids and leaving for a few days to sort things out."

Silence has given way to complete stillness. Not a breath… not a movement. We boys of summer had no comeback for this one.

"I guess I saw it coming and thought if I ignored it, the problems would go away. She would somehow overlook my inadequacies again and…"

"What inadequacies Mark?" came a cry from the brotherhood. "You seem like the rest of us… just one of the guys. You know, all kidding aside, we're pretty good husbands and stepfathers."

"Perhaps I am just like you, I don't know. But my wife is tired of me not communicating with her. I don't know why but I just can't talk to her about my feelings. It's not like we argue alot cause we don't. I honestly don't know how to express myself to her. I'm afraid to let her in… afraid she won't like what she sees when the real me is left out there hanging to dry."

"Has she left yet?" we asked.

"No, she was packing. She hadn't even told the kids yet."

"Call her back... Tell her to wait until you get home."

"But..."

"Do it Mark."

We spent the next few moments putting Mark back together. We told him to listen carefully to what his wife had to say and to ask for help in getting her needs met. And yes, we told Mark to forget about the weekend NBA Championship games and tell her he was prepared to go to the weekend retreat... We would tape the games for him!

We also told him to forget about his ego and let it all hang out in her presence regarding his fears about opening up to her. If that meant shedding a tear or sobbing like a baby, so be it. Just do it and be himself... not what his male ego image said he was suppose to be.

We circled the wagons and put our hands on his shaken shoulders.

We prayed for him.

We prayed with him.

We sent him on his way.

And then, we sat in silence...

Finally, Rob broke the ice... "Why are we so afraid to express ourselves to our wives? Everyone in this room cares deeply for his wife and his family. Kidding and male bonding aside, everyone in this room wants to please his wife. So why are we so afraid to let it all hang out in their presence? Why do we feel so compelled to maintain our male facade?"

The whistle blew. Tonight's game was over, yet probably not forgotten for a long time.

Thought for the Day: Who are our role models? As adult males, fathers, husbands, stepfathers, who do we look up to? Granted, we may watch and admire certain athletes, actors... maybe a politician or writer rolls down the pike every now and then. But, who do we really look up to when the show is over and the stadium lights have been turned off?

Find one.

And, by all means, don't lose sight of the Great One who walked this earth some 2000 years ago. He's alive today, and waiting to lead you to the FeatherZone.

There is a spiritual giant within each of us telling us we need not remain enslaved by weakness or victimized by frustrating limitations. The giant within you is always struggling to burst his way out of the prison you have made for him. Why not set him free today?
Norman Vincent Peale

It is wise to remember that a misplaced "I" can transform the marital relationship into a martial one...
Anonymous

Day # 350 "Flea Flicker..."

The greatest playground play ever diagrammed in the dirt... the old flea flicker. The quarterback raises up and fires a pass to the end, who has run a 7-yard curl pattern. The left halfback, or if you didn't have enough players to have a halfback the center would do, waits on the ball to leave the quarterback's hand... then darts behind the end, running at an angle up the field but towards the sidelines. The end, especially if he is good, doesn't even receive the ball. He catches it and simultaneously flips it to his teammate scampering down the sidelines as the defense has already closed in on the end for the tackle... or two-hand-touch if you cared about your bones. How many times we scored on that play...

My lovely teenage stepdaughters are running their version of the flea flicker on me. Just when I think I know who has the ball... in this case, the phone, they flea flicker it all the way down the field.

I finally concede a touchdown to them and wait for the kickoff to get the receiver. Boom! They've done it to me again... an on-sides kick and they have recovered it! Before I can cry foul or look for the referee's flag, they're off and running. This time I decide to blitz; I'm looking to cause a turnover. Wouldn't you know it! They've called a screen pass. There's so much interference out in front of them I don't stand a chance. Between call waiting, their beepers going off, and the number of scrawny little quarterbacks throwing passes their way, I feel... Defenseless is putting it mildly, and by the way, I know we didn't look that scrawny as teenagers did we? These kids look like they've never played a serious down of backyard football in their lives!

At least I can leave the "home cooking" beating I'm taking and run down to the pay phone. I crawl to my car, drive down to the pay phone a few blocks away, and... you guessed it — more teenagers on the phone, and not just one but an entire team. They may be the ones calling my house for all I know.

What to do? Well, the old man has a few trick plays of his own from that old and tattered playbook called experience. I drive up, ask them if they have any jumper cables... there's a carload of girls down the road with a dead battery... nice looking low rider they're in too, and...

Some things never change. They will take the fake on the old stop and go play every time.

Thought for the Day: Teens and telephones, men and TVbutt, women and... whatever (I punt on this one!). We all have our addictions... our "self-stims", and we all have our plays we call to confuse the opposition. Delay of game penalties don't dampen our creative spirits when we're in that "zone". We'll do whatever it takes short of cheating to steal a few more precious moments. From flea flickers to screen passes we'll call a variety of plays to get our way.

All fun and games in the course of a gameday, right? Perhaps, but the question we must ask ourselves is this... does our "addiction" and subsequent playcalling cause strife among the home team... the players that truly matter? There's only one way to find out. Ask... and do so with genuine concern in your heart, not with TVbutt in your hands.

When in doubt, call a timeout, walk over to the sidelines, and spend a few solitary moments with the Coach. He might refer you to His Playbook... what plays you'll find in Proverbs or one of Paul's letters, not to mention the four Gospels. And you thought the Four Horsemen were something special.

Happy is the man that findeth wisdom, and the man that getteth understanding. For the merchandise of it is better than the merchandise of silver, and the gain thereof than fine gold.
Proverbs 3:13-14

Whatsoever things are true, whatsoever things are honest, whatsoever things are just, whatsoever things are pure, whatsoever things are lovely, whatsoever things are of good report; if there be any virtue, and if there be any praise, think on these things... and the God of peace shall be with you.
Philippians 4:8-9

Day # 358 Male Bonding…

The bond that is evolving among the group is beyond words; well, maybe not that unbelievable, but well beyond the typical male bonding thing and certainly beyond all expectations. The guys are genuinely starting to care about each other, to care about their families… their communities.

Tonight we had a free-for-all, but not like several weeks ago when everybody was singing the blues. Tonight was fun night. Maybe we just needed a good laugh or two.

"I'll never forget my wife and I lying on the couch late one evening. The kids were in bed and we were both relaxed and in playful moods… too playful for the couch," laughed Joe. "Well, one thing led to another and before you know it I was naked to my knees when the kids' bedroom door opened. My wife knocked me to the floor, and I proceeded to pull my pants up while crawling halfway under the couch."

'What are you doing?' questioned my nine-year-old stepdaughter. 'Did you find my missing…'

"Oh, not yet, honey, but daddy's looking for it."

Men and their toys…

"We went for a Sunday dinner to my parents recently," chuckled Tom, "and when we got there Katie, my seven-year-old stepdaughter, ran up to her grandmother… 'Grandma,' Katie whispered, 'I love you more than my other grandma.'

'Don't tell her that now Katie,' my mom responded. 'You don't want to hurt her feelings.'

'Oh, I won't. When I'm with her I tell her the same thing.' "

We're beginning to understand how women operate.

"My six-year-old stepson stunned me the other night," said Billy. "I have a younger brother who occasionally comes by to shoot the breeze. He's a good guy but a little on the wild side, being single and all. Anyway, my little Joshua walked up to Tony and asked him a question… 'Uncle Tony, did you go to Sunday school when you were little?'

145

'You bet I did,' replied Tony.

'I'll bet,' Joshua sighed, 'that it wouldn't do me any good either.' "

Out of the mouths of babes...

"My stepson is just like his mom... an eternal optimist. Sometimes he even amazes me at how he can see the silver lining in the worst scenario," stated John. "He was playing a little league game the other day when a late arriving father asked my stepson, who was playing right field, what the score was."

" 'Eleven zip, top of the first,' yelled my stepson.

'Eleven to nothing?' questioned the man, 'and you're not upset?'

'Upset? No way!' yelled my boy with a gleam in his eye. 'We haven't batted yet!' "

Our kids... the stuff that dreams are made of...

I have an extended family here with these men. We hug, we cry, we holler and laugh, and sometimes sigh. In the end, we are all learning to love one another, to laugh at ourselves, and to grow from each other's strengths as well as shortcomings. There's an emerging sense of security in this group, a sense that we're a team here... all for one and one for all for the betterment of our children, our families, our brotherhood, and ourselves.

Thought for the Day: You cannot teach a man anything; you can only help him to find it within himself.

Galileo

The greatest revolution of our generation is the discovery that human beings, by changing the inner attitudes of their minds, can change the outer aspects of their lives.

William James

On the Path...

An incredible goodness is operating on your behalf.
Confidently receive God's abundance, prosperity, and the
best of everything. Expect great things to happen. God
wants to give you every good thing. Do not hinder His
generosity by disbelief.
Norman Vincent Peale

Day # 362 Just Another Year?

Thought for the Day: I have learned that success is to be measured
not so much by the position that one has reached, as by the obstacles
which he has overcome while trying to succeed.
Booker T. Washington

It's hard to imagine a year going by so fast and yet, so long. At times I didn't know if we would make it... to the end of the year that is, right dear?

It has been interesting to say the least, quite a change from living alone with virtually no responsibility.

I've been called more names this past year than at any other time in my life... from honey to heartless, darling to dad to derelict; from father to fatty to funny to frugal, and finally, from Joseph to jerk to Jamie's old man to just that man to just like all men. That's the printable names only.

I've had good days, bad days, dog days, delightful days. Some days I'll never forget, like the day a few weeks ago when I told the girls I'd like to adopt them. Some days I'd pay to forget, like the day my girls told me I was not their father and had no business in their lives. Somedays I truly can't remember if I forgot them or not.

I've seen teenagers come and teenagers go... short ones, tall ones, brown ones, crazy ones; one with no arms and no legs. In fact, he was at the house the first time I went over to Donna's to meet the kids. I let him drive my car in the church parking lot across the street. Donna knew at that point I was crazy enough to handle this family.

I've seen long-haired, hippie looking boys searching for Shannon and the same things I was searching for at their age — the meaning of life. I've seen no-haired, low ridin', jammin', slammin' boys not searching for anything more than their next ride and the whereabouts of Jamie at the mall.

I've been introduced to cows, pigs, goats and peacocks, horses and ponies up close and personal. I never knew a stable could smell so good.

I've felt things I have never felt before... from extreme anxiety to absolute exuberance, from tremendous loss to love beyond space and time. I've felt emotional pain so deep I thought the days could grow no darker. I've felt childlike joy beyond my wildest dreams.

Most of all, I've felt love... unconditional love.

And I've given love... unconditional love.

I've tasted fatherhood and I'm ready for seconds... another year.

I've tasted the utter joy of partnership with my wife, and I'm ready to share it for eternity.

God has blest me.

Prayer: Promise Yourself...
To be strong that nothing can disturb your peace of mind.
To talk of health, happiness and prosperity to every person you meet.
To make your friends feel that there is something in them.
To look on the sunny side of everything and make your optimism come true.
To think only of the best, to work only for the best, and expect only the best.
To be just as enthusiastic about the success of others as you are about your own.
To forget the mistakes of the past and press on to the great achievements of the future.

To wear a cheerful countenance at all times and have a smile for every living creature you meet.
To give so much time to the improvement of yourself that you have no time to criticize others.
To be too large for worry, too noble for anger, too strong for fear, and too happy to permit the presence of trouble.
To think well of yourself and to proclaim this fact to the world, not in loud words, but in great deeds.
To live in faith that the world is on your side so long as you are true to the best that is in you.

Author Unknown

Day # 365 Champions!

If you can imagine it, you can achieve it.
If you can dream it, you can become it.
William Arthur Ward

Who would have believed it? Six months ago I lay in bed wondering what the voices meant, "If you build it..." Four months ago I stood outside the "locker room" wondering if any brave souls would show for our first meeting.

Tonight we're meeting in a new clubhouse. The old one could no longer contain us. We're hosting the brotherhood from across town. Yea, that's right... an off-shoot of our original group. Word has it another group is forming. Look out AA! SFA is alive and growing...

Oh, did I mention? The men, the brotherhood... the "boys n' the hood" are having a potluck dinner tonight prepared totally by us. Quiche is on the menu. The local emergency room has been alerted. We've come a long way baby!

As we start, we gather in a circle, grown men glasping hands...
"God, grant me the serenity to..."

149

Let the games begin. We are stepfathers. We were born to be…

———————————

*If two of you shall agree on earth as touching anything
that they shall ask, it shall be done for them of my Father
which is in Heaven. For where two or three are gathered
together in my name there am I in the midst of them.*
Matthew 18:19-20

Day # 372 Father's Day…

A great man is he who has not lost the heart of a child.
Mencious

My second Father's Day on the calender but my first one with
meaning. I have the homemade Father's Day cards to prove it…

Happy Father's Day, Joe
*   Thanks for being there over the past year. I know joining this
family has been a trip. But I'm glad you did it. I really didn't like
you taking mom away from us. I felt abandoned. Now I know it
was the best thing in the world for her. You're good to her and good
to us too. I hope you have a great day.*
*   Love,*
*   Shannon*
P. S. Don't forget to leave me the car keys!

And from Jamie, my fifteen-year-old…

Hey Dad!
*   What's happening? Hope you enjoy your breakfast. I cooked*

*you pancakes like you cook me! Don't count fat grams today, okay...
It's your day to relax and eat and do what you want.*

*You've been a great father to me. I was so scared when mom
married you. I figured you would leave us after a few months, especially after me and Shannon stole your car. But you didn't! You're
always here and I'm glad. Mom's really happy too. I've never really
had a father I could count on before. Now, I finally got the one I
always wanted and needed.*

Happy Father's Day!

Love,
Jamie

Thought for Future Father's Days: *I Loved You Enough*
*Someday when my children are old enough to understand the logic
that motivates a mother and father, I will tell them...*

*I loved you enough to ask about where you were going, with whom,
and what time you would get home.*

*I loved you enough to be silent and let you discover that your hand-
picked friend was a creep.*

*I loved you enough to make you return a "Milky Way" with a bite
out of it to a drugstore and to confess, "I stole this."*

*I loved you enough to stand over you for two hours while you cleaned
your room, a job that would have taken me fifteen minutes.*

*I loved you enough to let you see anger, disappointment, disgust,
and tears in my eyes.*

I loved you enough to let you stumble, fall and get hurt.

*I loved you enough to let you assume responsibility for your actions
at six, ten, and sixteen.*

*But most of all, I loved you enough to say, "No" when you hated me
for it.*

That was the hardest part of all.

Author Unknown

151

"Your reason to be...."

Epilogue

your reason to be…

Feath-er-Zone: 1. Holden Beach, North Carolina... late September, low tide, sun rising in the east and full moon setting in the west... that glorious moment when night gives way to dawn's early light; two dolphin playfully swimming 50 yards off shore while the pelicans hover above, diving for breakfast. **2.** husband and wife walking hand in hand along the shoreline, their kids safely grown and making their own nests... both with the peace of mind knowing they will share paradise together for an eternity... a clear path to Home.

Thought for the Future...

One day, a feeling will hit you,
A spiritual feeling full of love and glee.
A vision so enlightening,
From that moment on life's a joy and you're free.
And playfully you float like a feather,
You soar like a leaf from a tree.
The things you swore you needed have faded
Your reason to be...

I found my reason to be on the path to the FeatherZone. I sometimes feel like I'm floating, especially when my vision is clear.

Yet, my ultimate destination is to spend eternity with my family in paradise. For the time I may have left on this earth, I'll settle for paradise at the beach. But, true eternal paradise will commence the day Jesus returns to take His people Home to meet God, our Heavenly Father... our Creator.

I can think of no greater gift to one's children than to lead them Home.

Your Reason to be...

Stepfathers' Anonymous Playbook II

We want your story!

Share your story or anecdote with the brotherhood of stepfathers around the globe! If you have a humorous, joyful, insightful, humble, heartwarming, etc... experience to share as a stepfather or perhaps as a child growing up in a stepfamily, send it to us. We're looking forward to publishing *Stepfathers' Anonymous Playbook II* in the near future.

Please send to:

Covenant Communications
P. O. Box 367
Old Hickory, TN 37138-0367
FAX: (615) 860-3601

We will make sure you, the author, are credited for the contribution, unless, of course, you wish to remain anonymous. We're excited about *SFA II*... We know many of you have a story or two to tell...

Please feel free to contact us if interested in setting up a Stepfathers Anonymous group in your area. Additional information regarding speaking engagements, newsletters, booklets, and workshops can also be obtained at the above address or by calling (615) 847-2066 or (800) 979-3882.

Keep the faith...

Order Form

I want to order _____ copies of *Stepfathers' Anonymous Playbook... The Season That Never Ends* for just $10.97/copy, plus shipping ($3 for first book; .75 for each additional book). I will also receive a complimentary issue of the monthly inspirational magazine, *Shepherd's Way* free with my book order.

Enclosed is my check or money order in the amount of _____ made payable to Covenant Communications. **Credit Card Orders Available! See enclosed flyer for 800# or call us for the 800# available to you. Orders taken 24 hrs / day!**

Please send my order to:

Name: _____

Street: _____

City/State/Zip: _____

Sales Tax: Please add 8.25% for books shipped to Tennessee addresses.

**Credit card orders: Call (800) 979-3882 — 24 hrs/day.
Your order will be shipped within the next business day.**

**Covenant Communications
P. O. Box 367
Old Hickory, TN 37138-0367
(615) 847-2066
(800) 979-3882**

Shepherd's Way

Spirit-filled & Common Sense Thoughts on Managing Ourselves & Our Flock

"**Shepherd's Way**, the best 'pick-me-up' magazine around."

"Very unique, yet down to earth with heart... I like the fact that I can read the quotes and ancedotes during those times of the day when I need a positive boost."

"I keep one in my car and read it in traffic jams!"

"**Shepherd's Way**, it makes me laugh... it makes me think, and I love the format. It's quick and to the point."

Get the message? Thousands of our regular readers get the **Shepherd's Way** message delivered to their doorstep every month. That's 12 issues for only $11.97! The best twelve bucks you'll spend all year... a wonderful gift to send a friend or loved one.

Clip and mail this coupon to: Covenant Communications, P.O. Box 367, Old Hickory, TN 37138 -0367

Yes! Enter my subscription to **Shepherd's Way for** one year for $11.97.

Canadian and foreign rates: $15.97 per year with order, US funds.

Name: _____

Address: _____

City: _____ State: _____ Zip: _____

☐ Payment enclosed   ☐ Please bill me
or order by phone at (800) 979-3882. We'll bill you later.

Request for Workshop / Presentation

If you or your organization are interested in a presentation by Joe & Donna Pritchard entitled **"The Stepparenting Playbook... How to Win at Home"**, please complete the following information request card and mail it in, or call us at Covenant Communications (615) 847-2066.

If you like the excerpts from the book, *Stepfathers' Anonymous Playbook... The Season That Never Ends*, you'll love their presentation! Come join the fun... but please leave your stepkids at home! This workshop is for adults only... Some of the techniques (plays) we introduce are not to fall into the hands of your children for fear they will use them on you!

Name / Organization: _____

Address: _____

City / State / Zip: _____

Phone: _____

Dates Available: _____

Comments: _____

Covenant Communications
P.O. Box 367
Old Hickory, TN 37138-0367
(615) 847-2066
(800) 979-3882

When the One Great Scorer comes to write against your name, He marks, not that you won or lost, but how you played the game.
Grantland Rice